STANDING UP COUNTRY

STANDING

UP COUNTRY

The
CANYON
LANDS
of
UTAH
and
ARIZONA

C. GREGORY CRAMPTON

RIO NUEVO PUBLISHERS
TUCSON, ARIZONA

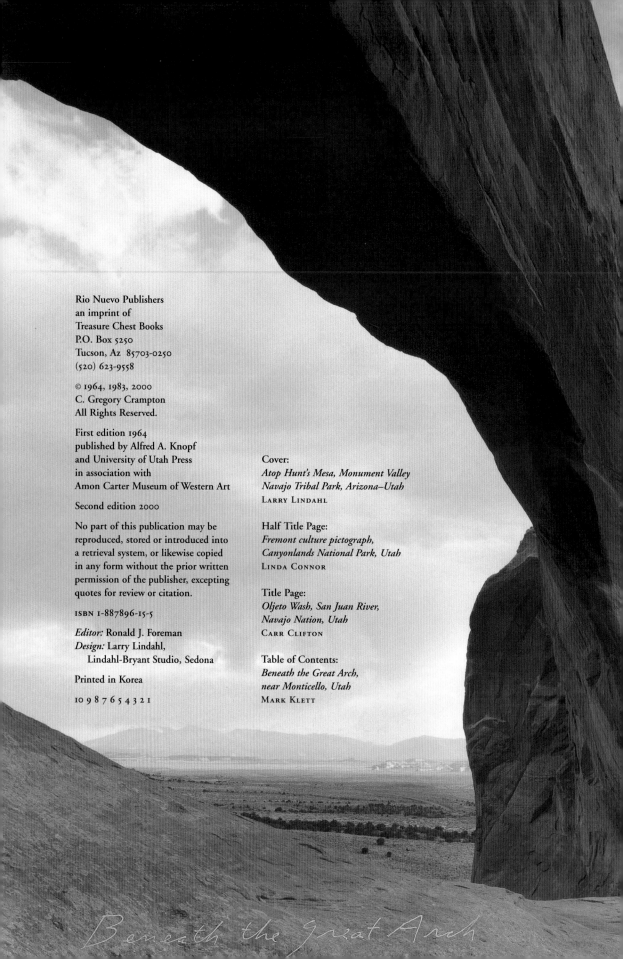

Rio Nuevo Publishers
an imprint of
Treasure Chest Books
P.O. Box 5250
Tucson, Az 85703-0250
(520) 623-9558

© 1964, 1983, 2000
C. Gregory Crampton
All Rights Reserved.

First edition 1964
published by Alfred A. Knopf
and University of Utah Press
in association with
Amon Carter Museum of Western Art

Second edition 2000

No part of this publication may be
reproduced, stored or introduced into
a retrieval system, or likewise copied
in any form without the prior written
permission of the publisher, excepting
quotes for review or citation.

ISBN 1-887896-15-5

Editor: Ronald J. Foreman
Design: Larry Lindahl,
    Lindahl-Bryant Studio, Sedona

Printed in Korea

10 9 8 7 6 5 4 3 2 1

Cover:
Atop Hunt's Mesa, Monument Valley
Navajo Tribal Park, Arizona–Utah
LARRY LINDAHL

Half Title Page:
Fremont culture pictograph,
Canyonlands National Park, Utah
LINDA CONNOR

Title Page:
Oljeto Wash, San Juan River,
Navajo Nation, Utah
CARR CLIFTON

Table of Contents:
Beneath the Great Arch,
near Monticello, Utah
MARK KLETT

Beneath the Great Arch

CONTENTS

near Monticello, Utah 6/21/82

Member of 1958-63 Glen Canyon historical survey and salvage team
C. Gregory Crampton

PREFACE

THIS BOOK IS A BIOGRAPHY of the elaborately carved sandstone canyon country of southeastern Utah and northeastern Arizona. Its recorded history—dating from 1776—is as old as the United States, yet for most Americans the region remained largely *terra incognita* until 1922, when representatives from seven western states signed the fateful Colorado River Compact.

My own acquaintance with this sculptured land dates back to 1941, when I drove the late Herbert E. Bolton on a trip from Berkeley, California, to Mexican Hat, Utah. Bolton believed that historians could improve the quality of their writing by being acquainted with the places about which they wrote. We reached Mexican Hat by way of Cameron, Tuba City, and Kayenta; we spent one night at Kayenta and were entertained with stories of the big sandstone country by Louisa Wade Wetherill. Glimpses of the mouth of the Tsegi, of Comb Ridge, Agathla, Hoskininni Mesa, Monument Valley, Alhambra Rock, Mexican Hat, and the stark and beautiful stream, the San Juan River, convinced me that I had to see more of this land. With Norman Nevills, Bolton went through the San Juan Canyon and stopped in Glen Canyon to make a reconnaissance of the Crossing of the Fathers before going on to Lee's Ferry. The data were incorporated in Bolton's edition of the diary of Friar Francisco Silvestre Velez de Escalante published as *Pageant in the Wilderness* (1950).

In 1945, I joined the staff of the Department of History, University of Utah, and thus came within close range of the canyon country. There followed trips to it with family and colleagues. Two years in a row I rafted through Glen Canyon. There were hours spent in libraries and with people who were familiar with the canyon lands. I found that the region had a history as rich as its matchless landscape, but no one had written about it in any comprehensive way. This was true up to 1956 when the Upper Colorado River Storage Act became law. That huge reclamation program was a culmination of forces that had taken shape by 1922 when the Colorado River Compact was signed. The construction of Glen Canyon Dam, one of the basic units of the project, would destroy valuable historical values in the canyon. When the National Park Service began to formulate plans for undertaking salvage studies in the area of the projected reservoir—to be called Lake Powell— I urged that adequate study be made of the historical remains jeopardized by this construction. I was indeed happy to accept responsibility for the supervision of the salvage studies in history, a pleasant and exciting task, undertaken through formal arrangements between the National Park Service and the University of Utah and completed in 1963. This was part of a comprehensive and thoroughgoing program of salvage that included archeology, ecology, and geology carried out by the University of Utah and the Museum of Northern Arizona.

In large measure, this book is an outgrowth of the historical fieldwork undertaken in the Glen Canyon region. During the course of these salvage studies I traveled through the canyons, through some of them several times, and became intimately familiar with much of the canyon country and generally acquainted with parts of it I had not known before. As these studies progressed, I drew plans for this work, one that would entirely encompass the great sculptured land, a land that is given a historical and geographical unity by the canyons and by the river that made them.

National awareness of the scenic beauty of the entire canyon country, practically non-existent before 1956, greatly accelerated as the dam took shape. Where hundreds had traveled before, thousands now boated through Glen Canyon to see some of the spectacular landscape before the impounded waters of Lake Powell drowned it. The governors of Utah and Arizona joined in. In a well-publicized trip in May 1962, they spent three days on the water in what was described as the "Governors' Farewell to Glen Canyon."

In 1963, after the gates had closed and the reservoir had begun to fill, the Sierra Club published a handsome folio volume, *The Place No One Knew: Glen Canyon on the Colorado,* containing seventy-two brilliant photographs in color and an essay on "The Living Canyon" by Eliot Porter. The book is an eloquent admission by one of our strongest conservation organizations that Glen Canyon and much of the red rock country on either side of it were all but unknown to those dedicated to the protection of the earth's natural scenic resources. Thus, when opposition to the dam builders might have been successful, few voices were heard.

Of course the canyon lands were known— and intimately by some—to pre-Columbian and modern Indians, Spanish friars, Mexican traders, government explorers, stockmen, miners, surveyors, river runners, archeologists, nature lovers, and dam builders, all of whose activities were detailed in the first edition of *Standing Up Country,* published in 1964.

The subsequent formation of Canyonlands National Park (1964) and Glen Canyon National Recreation Area (1965) sharpened the public focus, as did the upgrading of Arches and Capitol Reef from national monuments to national parks. Today, the public recognizes that this whole sweep of country is rich in history and is one of unparalleled grandeur—that it is indeed one of the earth's great places.

C. GREGORY CRAMPTON
St. George, Utah
June 1983

Delicate Arch, Arches National Park, Utah GEORGE H.H. HUEY

STANDING UP COUNTRY

SLICK-ROCK WILDERNESS

IF YOU FOLLOW the main-traveled roads through southeastern Utah and northeastern Arizona, you will be deceived. You will see places of great interest, but from the highways you will miss much of the wild and rugged scenery. You will scarcely become aware of the immensity of the canyon country or even that canyons and cliffs are its dominant topographical features. Much of the country looks flat and uninteresting, since the highways for the most part skirt the canyons, staying in the open reaches whenever possible. Dramatic landscapes like Capitol Reef, the Moab Valley, Comb Ridge, Monument Valley, Echo Cliffs, and Bryce Canyon are easily reached, but as you speed along on hard surface you may be missing far more than you see.

This is the heart of the great Colorado Plateau. The name is right, for this is rim rock country; its general surface is flat—a tableland. Approach from any direction and you will soon find yourself on a rim looking *down into* rather than *up at*. You can see for great distances. The skyline from nearly every vantagepoint is horizontal or nearly so. It may appear as a long, continuous line extending for many miles until it is lost in the distant haze. If you were to move toward the center you would observe, however, that the plateau in many places consists of a giant staircase descending from the edges toward the middle. There are several levels, each a platform or terrace of irregular width, sometimes extending for many miles. The platforms

Inspiration Point, Bryce Canyon National Park, Utah
KERRY THALMANN

commonly rise above one another in precipitous steps, in some places hundreds or even thousands of feet in height. The façade of cliffs, separating the terrace levels, appear as grand, majestic walls, murals, pilasters, and columns or as skirts and buttresses forming one of the most dramatic features in a dramatic landscape.

Water has thoroughly dissected the stupendous staircase, leaving separated segments of the terraces in the form of mesas, some of them many square miles in extent. Smaller remnants are detached and sculptured buttes, monuments, pinnacles, minarets, and standing rocks, in infinite variety. Very often the eroded remnants between the watercourses may be rounded forms covering sometimes square miles of surface. They may appear as knobs or as elongated hummocks in the close formation called "fins." They may be lumpy, bumpy forms like the grotesque figures in Goblin Valley. They rise in beautifully proportioned spires, usually in clusters, best seen in The Needles and the Land of Standing Rocks.

Steep-walled canyons dominate the landscape. The intricacy of the canyons increases as you approach the rivers that drain the entire region, though this may not be apparent from a distance. The angular character of the general topography tends to run together in horizontal lines. There are few of the broad, graceful, rounded contours of mountains and valleys commonly seen in humid climates. The intricately sculptured country looks like a tableland, but do not try to cross it unless you know your way. Move in a straight line toward the center of the canyon country from any direction and you will eventually find yourself standing at the precipice of a mesa or a canyon, contemplating a sheer, vertical drop of a hundred feet, a thousand feet or more. You can go no

Sandstone pedestal, Grand Staircase-Escalante National Monument, Utah John George

further; you have become "rim rocked," to use a good canyon-country term. You stand at the edge of the world and there before you lies a natural spectacle of surpassing magnificence. As W.C. McBride first observed in the June 1907 edition of Pacific Monthly, "There is as much country standing up as there is laying down."

Not all of the canyon country looks flat. Spectacular deviations break the horizontal plane in a number of places. Here and there the surface has been broadly warped, buckled, or folded to produce either gentle undulations in the surface or sharply plunging slopes, all of which have complicated the drainage pattern and influenced the formation of canyons.

The most dramatic departures are the huge laccolithic domes made of volcanic masses of rock that pushed up overlying sedimentary strata to great heights but never broke through them. The resultant steep surfaces eroded to form mountains of traditional appearance standing singly or in groups on top of the level platform of the plateau. Appropriately named "island mountains," they seem alone and out of place.

Wherever you stand in the canyon country, appearances are deceptive: at low elevations you are shut in by rock walls; at the upper levels you find that distant views, except for the laccolithic mountains, tend to flatten out. Only birds see the true face of the earth. The best introduction to the canyon country is to fly over it. A world unsuspected by the surface traveler comes into view: a marvelous, intricately carved and sculptured wilderness done in sandstone.

From the air you see the vertical dimension. Canyons cut deep in the bare slick rock seem to be everywhere below. The deep, narrow ones meander gracefully in sweeping curves, undercutting the walls and forming niches, alcoves, caves, grottos, glens, and amphitheaters. Occasionally a stream will break through a loop in an entrenched meander and leave a bridge or an arch of rock. A window may appear where water and wind have eroded through a thinning wall of stone.

There is scant vegetation except at the higher levels. Instead, the bare slick rock itself gives color to the landscape—red, orange, pink, chocolate, brown, purple, yellow, white, blue, green, and gray. Shades of red predominate. It colors the land, it reflects on and tints the clouds above, and it stains the water of the river that drains the land. The Spaniards had just the right name for this stream. They called it Colorado.

WEST SIDE

On the west the canyon country is sharply bounded by the lofty escarpments of the High Plateaus, which extend one hundred seventy-five miles from Bryce Canyon in the south to the Price River in the north. This great line of plateaus, ranging from eight thousand to more than eleven thousand feet in altitude, forms the divide between the Great Basin and the Colorado River. Bryce Canyon National Park lies along the rim of the Paunsaugunt Plateau, a huge, uplifted block more than nine thousand feet above sea level.

From the sharp rim at Bryce Canyon you look down into a forest of colorful rock laid bare by erosion. The short Bryce Creek, which heads in the maze of eroded pinnacles, is not characteristic of the canyons found along the main watercourses, but its parent, the Paria River, is.

The Paria, a tributary of the mighty Colorado River, quickly gathers its headwaters and flows south, through a succession of canyons it has carved in the White Cliffs, Vermilion Cliffs, and the jagged Cockscomb, a local name for the East Kaibab Monocline. After leveling out for a few miles along the Paria Plateau, the river drops into a deep gorge and finally reaches the Colorado just below Lee's Ferry. Buckskin Gulch, a main branch of the Paria, follows an even more spectacular course.

Bryce Canyon, the Paria River, and Buckskin Gulch help define the western edge of canyon country. Northeast of Bryce Canyon, the eleven-thousand-foot Aquarius Plateau dominates the skyline. Local names are used for its main segments—Table Cliff Plateau, Escalante Mountain, and Boulder Mountain. From the latter's lava-capped summit, half of the canyon country is visible. To Capt. C.E. Dutton of the Powell Survey, the view was "a sublime panorama…It is a maze of cliffs and terraces lined off with stratification, of rambling buttes, red and white domes, rock

platforms gashed with profound cañons, burning plains barren even of sage—all glowing with bright colors and flooded with sunlight."

Due south of Boulder Mountain, and running southeast from the base of the Table Cliff Plateau more than fifty miles to the Colorado River, are the long Straight Cliffs of the Kaiparowits Plateau. Northeast of the Kaiparowits Plateau and paralleling it is the remarkably intricate, meandering canyon of the Escalante River. Indeed, the entire watershed of the lower basin, almost denuded of soil, is one of the most elaborately sculptured parts of the canyon country. At the eastern base of Boulder Mountain is a twenty-five-mile-long elliptical depression, ringed by the inward-facing Circle Cliffs. Several tributaries of the Escalante originate in this depression and have carved a series of canyons through the western edge of the Circle Cliffs on their way to join the main river.

Bounding the Circle Cliffs on the east is the Waterpocket Fold, a high monoclinal ridge running continuously for eighty miles to the Colorado River and forming the backbone of Capitol Reef National Park. The Fremont River, which heads in the High Plateaus north of Thousand Lake Mountain, has cut a deep canyon through the Waterpocket Fold at Capitol Reef. The eastern slope of the Fold, a hogback boldly visible and deeply notched by erosion throughout its length, is a spectacle of great beauty.

East of Capitol Reef the Fremont River, kept in its course by sharp-rimmed mesas, flows through brightly colored country. Near Hanksville it comes out briefly into the open and picks up the Muddy Creek. The two join to form the Dirty Devil, which turns south, drops into a sinuous canyon, and flows to the Colorado.

Rising within this region—bounded by the Waterpocket Fold and the Fremont, Dirty Devil, and Colorado rivers—is a splendid group of five laccolithic peaks called the Henry Mountains. Three of them—Mt. Ellen, Mt. Pennell, and Mt. Hillers—stand close together, forming a range twenty miles long and as high as eleven thousand feet in elevation. The Henry Mountains, together with their counterparts on the east side—the La Sal and Abajo Mountains and Navajo Mountain—

comprise the highest peaks in the canyon country. They look like conventional mountains and, as all of them may be seen from great distances, they long have been landmarks in a country where the general horizon otherwise appears to be flat. The two southern peaks of the Henrys—Mt. Holmes and Mt. Ellsworth—are isolated from the main Henry range and from each other. Also known as the "Little Rockies," they rise about four thousand feet above Lake Powell in Glen Canyon, a few miles away.

Beyond Thousand Lake Mountain, the High Plateaus continue northward more than ninety miles to the high eastern rim of the Wasatch Plateau. Half a dozen streams, including the Price and San Rafael rivers, flow eastward off the Wasatch Plateau to water Castle Valley, a farming belt sixty miles long. The green areas of irrigated land stand out in sharp contrast to the gray soil and yellowish rock of adjacent mesas. Beyond, stretching for sixty miles north and south, is the remarkable San Rafael Swell. As the name suggests, it is an upwarp in the earth's surface, an elongated, kidney-shaped dome about twenty-five miles wide. Approach the Swell from any direction and you will encounter the distinctive hogback ridges that completely encircle it. The steep eastern and southern ridges comprise the San Rafael Reef. The inner face of this reef consists of cliffs ranging from hundreds to two thousand feet in height.

Within the encircling reefs, and rising gradually above them, is a gently domed open area dotted with low mesas, knobs, and rocks about ten miles wide and forty miles long, known as Sinbad. This recalls the Arabian Nights story of the second voyage of the traveler from Baghdad who was flown by the Roc to a "valley exceeding great and wide and deep, and bounded by vast mountains that spired high in the air." At either end, Sinbad is cut into mesas and steep canyons where it drains off to the San Rafael and Muddy rivers. After gathering together the creeks in Castle Valley, these two streams flow through spectacular canyons directly across the Swell.

The San Rafael River breaks across the steepest part of the San Rafael Reef and then flows through relatively open country to the Green River. The

Muddy emerges and, after passing through a barren but colorful landscape typified by the grotesque Goblin Valley, joins the Fremont to form the Dirty Devil.

Bounded by the San Rafael Reef and the Dirty Devil River on the north and west, and by the Green and Colorado rivers on the east and south, is the San Rafael Desert. Its surface is one of low relief with mesas, rounded knobs of stone, and occasional sand dunes that, oddly enough, are a rare sight in this sandstone country. Other unusual sights are extensive grass-covered areas and the soil-filled valley of the San Rafael.

The southern half of the San Rafael Desert is strikingly beautiful. A few miles south of Robber's Roost, the Land's End plateau narrows, abruptly breaks off, and then—in a series of irregular and magnificent steps—drops more than three thousand feet into the great gorges of the Dirty Devil and Colorado rivers. The Big Ridge, Red Benches, Orange Cliffs, and Black Ledge support terraces

of varying widths, frequently surmounted by spectacular remnants and elaborately dissected by deep, straight-walled canyons. That portion of the plateau between Happy Canyon, draining into the Dirty Devil, and Millard Canyon, draining into the Green River, is indeed one of the most thoroughly eroded areas in the entire canyon country. The Maze and Land of Standing Rocks are parts of it. The view from Panorama Point and neighboring overlooks in the northern reaches of Glen Canyon National Recreation Area, across to the rugged terrain of Canyonlands National Park, is one of exceptional grandeur.

Bounding the canyon country on the north is the high, southern escarpment of the Tavaputs Plateau. This, said Maj. John Wesley Powell in 1895, is "one of the most wonderful façades of the world." It is actually a sinuous escarpment up to fifteen miles wide and consists of the Book Cliffs, topped by the Roan Cliffs. This topographical feature, winding like a two hundred fifteen-mile-

San Rafael Swell at San Rafael River, Utah TOM TILL

long inverted "S," runs on an east-west axis from Castle Gate in Utah to Grand Mesa in Colorado.

From the ten-thousand-foot crest, the descent on the north to the Uinta Basin is gradual. On the south, the descent is rapid through a weird, barren labyrinth of short, steep canyons, lined with cliffs, mesas, sharp ridges, and isolated rocks.

EAST SIDE

Even in the heart of canyon country, where canyon, mesa, and slick rock dominate the landscape, there is some open country. Soft soil in some depth occurs and streams run in open courses. One such area is the continuous open lowland between Price and Grand Junction at the base of the Book Cliffs. This is the route of both a major highway and the Southern Pacific Railroad between Denver and Salt Lake City.

South of the Book Cliffs, between the Green River and Arches National Park, there is a huge wedge of country that is structurally similar to the Green River Desert Plateau. As you travel south over this wedge the topography becomes increasingly dramatic. As the Green and Colorado rivers flow toward their confluence, their canyons become deeper and broader.

From Gray's Pasture, Grand View Point, and the detached Junction Butte in Canyonlands National Park, you can look out over an eroded landscape of incomparable beauty. Matching these distant views are those close at hand. At Grand View Point, the land drops away more than a thousand feet to the broad White Rim. See how the rivers' tributaries have cut canyons through the rim. Weird and fantastic white-capped pillars of sandstone give Monument Canyon its name.

Adjacent to Gray's pasture, Upheaval Dome is a multi-colored, eroded, conical dome surrounded by a ring-like syncline about two miles in diameter. Erosion has broken through the northwestern section of the ring and this forms the head of Upheaval Canyon, which empties into the Green River, five miles away. Once called Christmas Canyon Dome, it has been characterized by E.T. McKnight of the U.S. Geological Survey as "the most peculiar structural feature that has yet been found in southeastern Utah."

The view from the Utah State Park at Dead-Horse Point matches that of the high places overlooking the confluence of the two rivers. This point is on the high rim of the plateau overlooking the Colorado River more than eighteen hundred feet below. Look off to the southwest past Grand View Point. You can see in profile the eroded valley of the Colorado for many miles. Nowhere can the horizontal and vertical lines of the canyon country be seen with greater ease. Toward the east stand the lofty La Sal Mountains, one of the laccolithic groups.

Arches National Park is well named. More than eighty stone arches and large windows in huge slabs of vertical rock have been counted in the monument. Some of these are so prominently displayed that they may be seen from the highway north of Moab, as far as nine miles away. But there is far more to the park than the arches. Cliffs, spires, alcoves, balanced rocks, fins, and other formations common to the canyon country abound, but there is also a difference. Features are spaced widely apart, so you can catch you breath between them. In the country to the west and south, the concentration of scenery can be overwhelming.

Southeast from Arches National Park, the Colorado runs through a canyon at the base of the La Sal Mountains. Where it opens out in the Richardson Amphitheater and Castle Valley, there are the exquisitely eroded Fisher Towers together with buttes, mesas, and other characteristic canyon-country formations. Downstream in a red-walled valley adjacent to the Colorado River is the town of Moab. South from Moab to the foot of the Abajo Mountains and west to the Colorado River is another wedge-shaped, dramatic sandstone landscape. Largely drained by streams that head on the slopes of the Abajo Mountains and the Elk Ridge, flowing northwest to the Colorado, the crescendo of intricate erosion is reached among the branches of Indian Creek, Salt Creek, and Butler Wash.

The best way for you to see this unbelievable landscape is to take a low-altitude flight over it. The upper-middle reaches of these watercourses are scarcely distinguishable as such: an incredible maze of canyons, and canyon compounded upon

Balanced Rock, Arches National Park, Utah George H.H. Huey

canyons, covers many square miles. Here is found
the greatest profusion of arches in the entire
canyon country outside Arches National Park.

Turn westward toward the Colorado, where
the country opens up a bit, and you a flying over
The Needles. Rows and clusters of rounded spires
stand above small grassy parks and parallel The
Grabens Valley, not far from the head of Cataract
Canyon. Across the river, only a few airline miles
away, is the Land of Standing Rocks.

The Abajo Mountains are a compact group
of laccolithic origin that dominates the skyline for
miles around. Half a dozen peaks range upwards
of eleven thousand feet above the base of the
group. One of the "island mountains," like the
La Sals to the north and Ute Mountain and the
Carrizos visible to the southeast in Colorado and
Arizona, respectively, the green-sloped Abajos
stand high above and in sharp contrast to the
great sandstone canyon country to the west.

Immediately to the west of the Abajos is the
deeply dissected Elk Ridge. Twenty miles long on
a north-south axis, this upland towers above and
broods over the profound Gypsum Canyon and
Dark Canyon, which have cut deeply into its steep
western face. Indeed, Dark Canyon is the greatest
of the tributary canyons of the entire region. From
its head to its mouth near the foot of Cataract
Canyon, a distance of about twenty-five miles,
there is a fall of five thousand feet. The heads of
Dark Canyon have almost cut Elk Ridge in two.
A very narrow place known as The Notch separates
North Elk Ridge from South Elk Ridge.

Drive up the dirt road to the Bear's Ears for
one of the grandest of panoramic views in the
canyon country. The ears are two huge buttes
over four hundred feet high standing on the rim
of South Elk Ridge, itself over eight thousand
feet in elevation. From a distance, the buttes
faintly resemble the ears of a bear. They are one

of the most prominent landmarks in the Four Corners country.

Look off the east and let your eye swing around the horizon to the south-southeast. You have just seen parts of four states. The San Juan Mountains, Mesa Verde, Ute Mountain in Colorado, and the Carrizo Mountains in northeastern Arizona form the skyline. Spread out in the foreground is the Sage Plain, which appears to be flat lowland. Actually, numerous northern canyon tributaries of the San Juan River gash this "plain." Here are McElmo Creek and Montezuma Canyon, where prehistoric peoples lived and built substantial dwellings, including those preserved at Hovenweep National Monument along the Utah/Colorado line. On the opposite side of the river, a broad country of scattered mesas, sand dunes, and shallow canyons at the base of the Carrizos falls away toward the San Juan River and Chinle Creek, which empties into the San Juan at Comb Ridge.

Now let your eye swing south to the Monument Valley Upwarp, a broad, high land sloping off to the east and west topped by the pinnacles that give Monument Valley its name. Closer at hand is the immense Grand Gulch Plateau. Bounding it on the east is the one-thousand-foot-high Comb Ridge, a sharply upturned monocline that runs one hundred miles from South Elk Ridge to Kayenta on the Navajo Nation in Arizona. Water drains from the eastern slope of the plateau and is deflected by this ridge into Comb Wash, which flows south to the San Juan. The highest branch of the Wash has nibbled away at a corner of the southeastern shoulder of South Elk Ridge to form the bright orange sandstone Arch Canyon.

White-rimmed Grand Gulch drains the western slope of the plateau. Its upper tributaries eat into the base of Elk Ridge and quickly drop into straight-walled canyons. These gather together to form a one-thousand-foot-deep main canyon— a narrow, meandering trench until it reaches the San Juan. The Grand Gulch Primitive Area is only accessible from a trailhead, located on Highway 261 four miles south of its junction with Highway 95. Off to the southwest is the long line of Clay Hills and Red House Cliffs.

Now turn west from your vantagepoint at Bear's Ears. You are at the head of White Canyon. Almost within sight below are the three stone bridges of Natural Bridges National Monument. Two of them bridge White Canyon. The third and largest bridge crosses Armstrong Canyon, a tributary. White Canyon is actually a narrow, straight-walled, but shallow watercourse at the base of a larger, open valley bordered by red cliffs and mesas. Highway 95, Utah's Bicentennial Highway, follows the course of this valley and provides access to the northern end of Lake Powell. The Highway 95 bridge at Hite is the only one to cross the Colorado River between Glen Canyon Dam and Moab. Riotously colorful Red Canyon, a few miles to the south, parallels White Canyon but is separated from it by cliffs that are impassable, save at one point called, appropriately, Blue Notch.

Bordered by Red Canyon and the Colorado River on the east and northwest and by the Clay Hills and San Juan River Arm of Lake Powell on the south is another wedge, sometimes called the San Juan triangle or Red Rock Plateau. Deep canyons slice through the whole knobby, bumpy, slickrock. The northern part is drained by the long and beautiful Moki, Cedar, and Lake canyons, which empty into the Colorado, and by Castle Creek flowing to the San Juan. Beyond Lake Canyon and the lower reaches of Castle Creek, a number of short, straight-walled canyons pitch off the steep slopes of Nokai Dome and Grey Mesa.

Some of the roughest terrain in the entire canyon country can be found south of the San Juan River in the Navajo Nation. Between Chinle Valley on the east and Navajo Mountain on the west, Gypsum Creek, Oljeto Wash, Copper Canyon, Nokai Canyon, Piute Creek, and lesser streams have cut back into the lofty tablelands astride the Utah-Arizona boundary. Piute, Nokai, No Man's, Skeleton, Zilnez, and Hoskininni mesas—all ending in shear, impassable, north-facing cliffs—are separated from each other by profound and highly colored canyons.

Much better known is the open country between Copper Canyon and Hoskininni Mesa, and the long, serrated Comb Ridge that arcs from the San Juan above Mexican Hat to Kayenta. Several high remnants—including Monitor Mesa, Boot Mesa, and Train Rock—stand in isolation. The whole climaxes in Monument Valley, where a cluster of isolated rock pillars tower a one thousand feet above the desert floor. Midway between Monument Valley and Kayenta, Agathla Peak—a volcanic neck also known as El Capitan— thrusts thirteen hundred feet into the air.

The gigantic rounded dome of Navajo Mountain, located on the edge of Glen Canyon just below the mouth of the San Juan, is the grandest natural edifice in the southern end of the canyon country. It is a single laccolite that rises to more than ten thousand feet in elevation. It may be seen from one hundred miles away. From its summit, much of the canyon country can be seen.

Stand on the western side of the peak and look northwest toward the long, extended fingers of the Kaiparowits Plateau. From here you can see the Colorado River, nine air miles and seven thousand feet lower in elevation. The whole mountain is heavily eroded on every side but particularly so on the northern and western sides. Steep, rugged canyons line the slopes, plunging toward the San Juan and the Colorado. Forbidding Canyon gathers the drainage from the southern slopes and from most of the western side and carries it in Aztec Creek to the Colorado. Walk down a short distance on the western slope of the mountain. Look carefully and you will be able to see the canyon of Bridge Creek. The great, vaulting arch of stone that spans the creek is Rainbow Bridge.

South and west of Navajo Mountain is the Rainbow Plateau, a huge triangle formed by Aztec Creek, the Colorado River, and the lower part of Navajo Canyon. The dominant feature is flat-topped Cummings Mesa, tilting toward the Colorado and cut into almost inaccessible parts by the deep, slot-like canyons emptying into the river. Between Cummings Mesa and Navajo Canyon, the country opens out but is dotted with isolated remnants like the stately Tower Butte and the massive Leche-e Rock.

South and east of Navajo Mountain, water from Navajo Canyon, Begashibito, and Shonto washes and Piute and Laguna creeks, flow west to the Colorado, north to the San Juan, and south

to the Little Colorado. Navajo Canyon is a long, narrow trench with a few side canyons. The upper tributaries have bitten into the plateau, separating the headwaters of Navajo Creek, Piute Creek, and Begashibito Wash, and in places only a narrow divide remains. Begashibito and Shonto washes slope gradually toward the southwest and are much less entrenched, although Shonto Canyon at Shonto is beautiful. The Shonto drainage heads on a divide overlooking the deep Keet Seel and other canyons that have been cut into the back of Skeleton Mesa. They unite to form the highly colored Tsegi Canyon whose stream, Laguna Creek, flows northeast from Marsh Pass through Kayenta to Chinle Wash. These intricate canyon systems offered homelands to prehistoric people, who built

Intact Ancestral Pueblo kiva, San Juan County, Utah
GEORGE H.H. HUEY

masonry dwellings in a number of places within them. Three have been preserved as units of Navajo National Monument: Betatakin in Tsegi Canyon, Keet Seel in the Tsegi's Keet Seel Canyon branch, and Inscription House, which is located in Navajo Canyon and is closed to the public.

The southern extension of the canyon country, as we have defined it, is reached at White Mesa. Standing alone on top of Kaibito Plateau, its white eastern and northern escarpments are visible for many miles, White Mesa tilts to the northwest and drains, through a network of beautiful white canyons, largely into Kaibito Creek in Choal Canyon and into the Colorado through Navajo Canyon. To the east of White Mesa, separated by the Kletha Valley, is the brooding bulk of Black Mesa. West is open country to the Echo Cliffs, a long, high, monoclinal ridge, an almost unbroken line of cliffs from near Moenkopi Wash to Lee's Ferry, where the Colorado has cut a gorge through them. Returning to Lee's Ferry, where the Paria enters the Colorado, we have come full circle.

THE RIVERS AND THE CANYONS

At Moab the Colorado River makes a dramatic entrance to the canyon country, flowing through The Portal, a gate in the eight hundred-foot-high cliffs at the head of a canyon two hundred seventy-nine miles long. After receiving from both sides the waters from the tributary canyon wilderness we have just explored, it ends just above Lee's Ferry, where the river makes and equally dramatic exit through a great gorge in the Echo Cliffs. This long canyon is not the same everywhere; descriptive names have been given to sections of it. There are other canyons of the Colorado. Above Moab the river and its tributaries—most notably the Dolores—pass through canyons, and below Lee's Ferry the river enters Marble Canyon and connects with the Grand.

From The Portal to the mouth of the Green River, a distance of sixty-two river miles, the Colorado flows in a canyon, sometimes called Utah's Grand Canyon, and drops one foot every mile throughout the entire distance. The river meanders leisurely as if to permit those who ride its surface to enjoy to the fullest the scenic beauties it has created. Much of the way, the cliff walls bordering the river are low, permitting views of flat-topped mesas in the distance. Continuing downstream, you will observe that more streams come from the left. Kane Springs Canyon, Lockhart Canyon, Indian Creek, and Salt Creek head back on the La Sal and Abajo mountains and the high country in between. For twenty miles above Lockhart Canyon, open basins near the river permit you to see the outlying ramparts of Hatch Point Mesa. On the right side, tributary canyons are short, heading on the high plateau between the Colorado and the Green that tilts toward the north, away from the river. Thirty-two miles downstream from The Portal, Dead Horse Point towers over eighteen hundred feet above the great bend known as The Gooseneck. Below the mouth of Indian Creek, the river canyon gets deeper, tributaries enter through narrow, slot-like canyons, and you are no longer afforded views of distant mesas. At the confluence of the Green and Colorado, the walls shoot up about thirteen hundred feet from the water's edge.

By the time the Green River reaches its mouth, it already has traveled through Lodore, Whirlpool, and Split Mountain canyons in the Uinta Mountains, and Desolation and Gray canyons that bisect the Ravaputs Plateau. The Green River comes out of Gray Canyon in the Book Cliffs above the town of Green River and flows through an open valley before it enters Labyrinth and Stillwater canyons.

The names are suggestive. The river drops only about one and a half feet every mile and, like the Colorado, it meanders after leaving the town of Green River, taking one hundred seventeen miles to reach its mouth—about half that many miles away as the crow flies. The general surface of the land itself tilts toward the north, so the canyon becomes deeper toward the south. Labyrinth Canyon begins its winding course below the mouth of the San Rafael River. At the head of Stillwater the canyon broadens out. In the vicinity of Millard Canyon, you may see on either side the straight walls of the Red Rim. But these soon disappear from view as you drop into an inner canyon below the white rim. The cliff walls grow higher and the canyon becomes narrower until the mouth is reached.

The Colorado and Green rivers flow placidly and leisurely before they converge, but then the Colorado enters forty-mile-long Cataract Canyon and its character changes abruptly. The river drops four hundred twenty-five feet, more than ten and a half feet per mile, and there are more than forty rapids. Cataract is the deepest canyon in Utah. Thirteen hundred feet deep at its head, it is more than two thousand feet deep near its mouth. The walls are steep, irregular slopes composed of many ledges and few high, massive cliffs, giving the

Cataract Canyon on the Colorado River, Glen Canyon National Recreation Area, Utah KAREN HALVERSON

canyon a ragged look not seen elsewhere in the canyon country.

Only a few short and steep canyons enter Cataract on the north side, but several come in from the high country to the south. Butler Wash in Red Lake Canyon and Cross Canyon enter Cataract near its head and drain much of The Needles country. Gypsum and Dark canyons are profound gorges that have eaten their way far back into Elk Ridge. Rowdy and Sheep canyons dissect the high plateau on either side of Dark Canyon.

Cataract Canyon has been partly drowned by Lake Powell. At maximum level the reservoir reaches about five miles above Gypsum Canyon to a point approximately one hundred eighty-seven miles above Glen Canyon Dam. For all of that distance, the course of the Colorado River may be traced in a general way by the line of cliffs that intermittently protrude above the waters of the lake. Narrow Canyon, seven miles long between Cataract and the mouth of the Dirty Devil, holds the lake within its walls, which are much lower than the cliffs of Cataract. A long,

narrow and winding arm of Lake Powell marks the inner channel of the Dirty Devil and the beginning of Glen Canyon.

From the mouth of the Dirty Devil to Lee's Ferry, a distance of one hundred seventy miles, the river once flowed quietly with intermittent stretches of fast water. There was nothing to compare with the pounding rapids of Cataract. Most of the way, the river flowed between beautiful, massive walls. Many tributaries entered through deep, narrow canyons, often not wide enough to permit human passage. Caves, grottos, glens, alcoves, and amphitheaters broke the monotony of majestic cliffs. The serenity of the water and peacefulness of the landscape suggested to Powell the name Glen Canyon.

Today, boat launching points at Lake Powell tell us where early visitors could most easily approach Glen Canyon. North Wash and Trachyte Creek, as well as White and Red canyons on the south side, were the main routes by which you could reach the upper part of the canyon. Near the mouth of Trachyte Creek, Hite was the only settlement in Glen Canyon, but it boasted a post office. Bullfrog Creek and Hall's Creek offered approaches into the river midway between Hite and the mouth of the San Juan.

Below Hall's Crossing, the canyon becomes deeper and crosses the Waterpocket Fold. One of the greatest sights in this sector is the Rincon, a huge, once-hanging meander of the Colorado that is now on the shore of Lake Powell. The narrow, winding course of the lake below indicates the depth of the canyon that was one thousand feet deep at the mouth of the Escalante River and Hole-in-the Rock Crossing.

If you exclude the Little Rockies of the Henry Mountains, the dominant feature of the landscape adjacent to Glen Canyon, between Hite and the San Juan, is the clean-swept, bare rock.

It is rather common in the canyon country to find streams that pay very little attention to existing topography. They seemingly flow about at will, not stopped by obstacles in their path. These are antecedent streams. They were there first, and as the present land forms rose in their paths, the streams simply cut a passage through them, The San Juan River is a striking example. It heads in southwestern Colorado, finds an open course through the corner of northwest New Mexico and the southeastern corner of Utah until it reaches Bluff. Just below there, it has sawed right through Comb Ridge. It comes out in the open briefly to receive Comb and Chinle washes and then enters the precipitous meandering canyon that has eroded at right angles to the wide Monument Upwarp. A few miles farther it does come to the surface briefly at Mexican Hat. Here the strangely eroded Valley of the Gods and the starkly beautiful Lime Creek amphitheater open out on the north. Beyond Mexican Hat, the San Juan winds about in The Goosenecks, the best-known and most accessible entrenched meander in the canyon country. From Chinle Creek the San Juan, in a canyon most of the way, used to flow a distance of one hundred thirty-three miles to the Colorado and dropped about nine hundred fifty feet. The steepest part was below Piute Farms, where the river tumbled over some rapids caused by boulders washed into the river from the tributaries heading on the high mesas along the Utah-Arizona line and on Navajo Mountain on the south side. Nokai Dome and Grey Mesa on the north side look down on a narrow lake today where once there was a deep river canyon.

During the days of river running, nearly everyone agreed that the most spectacularly beautiful section of Glen Canyon was below the San Juan, where the Colorado ran between the Kaiparowits Plateau and Grand Bench on the north shore, and Navajo Mountain and Cummings Mesa on the south shore. For thirty-five miles, towering walls rose on either side of the river. You could see the outliers of the Kaiparowits Plateau, and isolated remnants of the Cummings Mesa and Grand Bench, set back from the rims and drained by narrow, sinuous, and slot-like canyons.

Below West Canyon and Last Chance Creek, the river came out into more open country and the canyon walls diminished in the vicinity of the Crossing of the Fathers. Lake Powell now reaches its greatest width there. Glen Canyon Dam now stands a few miles "downstream," in a canyon nearly seven hundred feet deep.

Now walk out on the highway bridge at the dam and look downstream. There you see a remnant of Glen Canyon, little changed. But the river is now entirely subject to the control of man. In its freer days and swollen with spring runoff, the Colorado would sweep through a narrow defile through one-thousand-foot-high Echo Cliffs, spread out and calm down a bit at Lee's Ferry, and then join forces with the waters of the Paria River before dropping swiftly into Marble Canyon.

This canyon country above Lee's Ferry is a big land. For centuries, men have been working their way through this great country, taking its measure: loving it, cursing it, gutting it, changing it, enduring it, and leaving their mark upon it.

2

THE MYTHICAL RIVER

CROSSING OF THE FATHERS

SPAIN NEVER SENT more than a handful of
explorers into the great canyon country of Utah
and Arizona, but those few left a definite and
lasting imprint. They arrived late, near the end
of the Spanish era, long after their predecessors
had discovered and named the Colorado River.
In August 1540, less than two decades after Hernán
Cortés conquered the Aztec Empire in Mexico, a
naval expedition led by Hernando de Alarcón first
encountered the river at its mouth in the Gulf of
California. Later that year, a detachment from the
Francisco Vásquez de Coronado entrada—led by
don García López de Cárdenas—became the first
Europeans to peer down at the Rio Colorado
from the rim of the Grand Canyon.

Before the end of the sixteenth century, the
land traversed by Vásquez de Coronado was
colonized and brought securely under the Spanish
banner. The newcomers named this land New
Mexico because they thought it might rival in
wealth the homeland of the Mexicans and the
Aztecs. With great enterprise, Juan de Oñate,
colonizer and first governor, toured his realm from
the Great Plains to the lower Colorado, studying
the numerous Pueblo communities and looking
for mines. He also hoped to uncover some
information about a strait connecting the Atlantic
and Pacific oceans, believed to exist somewhere
not far north of New Mexico.

Indeed, the quest for a satisfactory water route
through the continent impelled much of the early

*Padre Bay on Lake Powell, Glen Canyon National
Recreation Area, Utah* GEORGE H.H. HUEY

exploration of North America. Christopher Columbus had sought a route west by sea to India, but discovered that America was in the way. For three centuries men would keep looking for either a sea-level passage to the Pacific or a pair of navigable rivers separated by a short land bridge.

Oñate retired from New Mexico without having found a strait or a river connection with the coasts. After his time the province settled down to a more routine existence, and few other adventurous quests were made into the unknown lands beyond its borders. In 1680, the bloody Pueblo Revolt forced the Spanish to abandon New Mexico, but Diego de Vargas restored the crown's authority eleven years later.

During the eighteenth century, there was a revival of exploration. For one thing, the Spanish found it necessary to defend their realm in North America against European rivals. In New Mexico, by mid century, the Spaniards established friendly relations with the Utes. This enabled traders and prospectors to work north from Santa Fe across the upper San Juan Basin and to reach the Colorado River by way of the Dolores and Gunnison rivers. There is little evidence to suggest that they ventured into the intricate canyon country of the lower San Juan and Colorado south and west of the La Sal Mountains, however.

Marble Canyon with Vermilion Cliffs in the distance, photographed during 1871-72 Powell Survey
JOHN K. HILLERS

During this same period, more imaginative explorers sought ways to connect with roads the widely separated Spanish frontier provinces in California, New Mexico, Texas, and Louisiana. Among these, two Franciscan priests from Santa Fe earned enduring fame. In 1776, Francisco Atanasio Domínguez and Francisco Silvestre Velez de Escalante—of the Order of Friars Minor—sought and obtained permission to find an overland route that could link Santa Fe with the mission in Monterey, California. They also hoped to find sites for new settlements, presidios, and missions. They left Santa Fe at the end of August and returned to New Mexico five month later.

Practically speaking, the expedition was a complete failure. In every other respect, it was a magnificent achievement.

The Franciscans and their party of thirteen made a great circle tour, a pioneer trip that kept them out of the canyon country until they neared the end of their journey. They traveled known trails north from Santa Fe to the Colorado River in western Colorado. Then they swung west over ground new to Spain, traveling through the Uinta Basin and reaching the Great Basin at Utah Lake. From there, they moved south to the latitude of Monterey, which they expected to follow west. But by then winter was approaching, so they decided to return to Santa Fe. They continued traveling south along the westward side of a long mountain range and, where the range tapered off, they turned east and headed across what is now the Arizona Strip.

With only vague information and without an Indian guide, they stayed in the open country, avoiding the few canyons that dropped south to the Colorado, and keeping in sight of the Vermilion Cliffs on their left. In late October, they reached the Colorado River at its confluence with the Paria River, which they called Rio Santa Teresa. Nearly a hundred years later, John D. Lee would establish Lee's Ferry at this same point.

Domínguez and Escalante christened their campsite San Benito Salsipuedes—the last word roughly translating to: Get out if you can! They undoubtedly felt boxed in, for here the Colorado River ran swift, deep, and cold. Downstream, the yawning mouth of Marble Canyon blocked their way. They looked into the deep mouth of Glen Canyon, with the towering Echo Cliffs on either side. Attempts to ford the river and to paddle across it on crude rafts failed. In desperation, they went upstream to look for another place to cross.

The first days of November were among the worst of their entire trip. The party managed to clamber up over the Echo Cliffs and headed northeast, wading through forty miles of salmon-pink sand. It began to rain, then snow, and then hail. Food was scarce, and soon they were reduced to eating cactus pads with crushed berry sauce. They finally reached the edge of Glen Canyon, only to find the river nearly five hundred feet below. No crossing was possible, so they went on.

"Doubtless God disposed that we should not obtain a guide, perhaps as a benign punishment for our sins," Escalante wrote in his diary. Even as he wrote these words, however, one of the men scouted ahead and found a passage down to the river through a short side canyon. The river at the canyon mouth was wide but not too deep. To keep the animals from losing their footing descending the canyon's steep slope, the party chopped steps into the sandstone.

Arriving at the river, they tested the bottom and found the water shallow enough to wade. The padres rode across on horseback, and by five o'clock in the afternoon of November 7 the entire party had forded the Colorado. They celebrated, wrote Escalante, "by praising God our Lord and firing off a few muskets as a sign of the great joy which we all felt at having overcome so great a difficulty." They named the ford La Purísima Concepción de la Virgin Santsima, but it will be forever known as the Crossing of the Fathers.

From the Colorado the trail to Santa Fe was comparatively easy. They struck off southeast across open but rocky country. The blue, rounded dome of Navajo Mountain bore northeast. Crossing Navajo Canyon where Kaibito Creek comes in and holding southeast, they headed the southern tributaries of Navajo Creek, passing White Mesa on their right. On November 12, they reached open trail and were out of the canyon country altogether. It was smooth traveling now by way of the Hopi and Zuni villages. They arrived back in Santa Fe on January 2, 1777.

Where the way was difficult for the Spaniards, thousands now live, work, and play. Highway 89

Crossing of the Fathers, Glen Canyon, Utah, ca. 1950s TAD NICHOLS

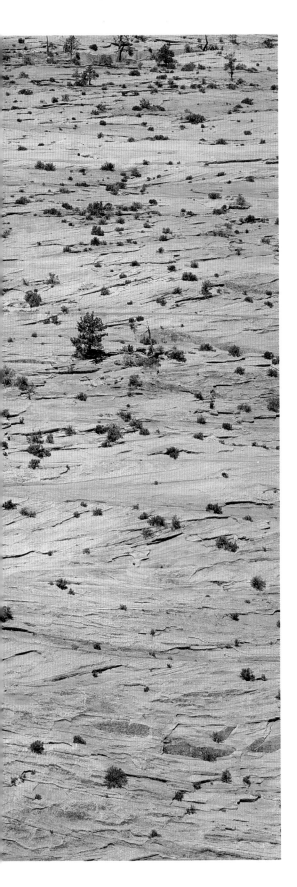

now crosses their trail from the Echo Cliffs to Padre Canyon, and a modern bridge spans the canyon that the friars found so forbidding. Padre Canyon with its stone steps and the Crossing of the Fathers are now submerged four hundred fifty feet beneath the waters of Lake Powell, but the place names remain to commemorate the first Europeans to tackle the canyon country.

SAN BUENAVENTURA

Domínguez and Escalante "discovered" the canyon country, but Alexander von Humbolt was the first to really put it on the map. The Spanish explorers made remarkable contributions to knowledge: Theirs was the first traverse of the Colorado Plateau and Great Basin by Europeans. Escalante's diary and expedition cartographer Bernard de Miera y Pacheco's maps provided fundamental information about plant life, animals, minerals, land, weather, and the location and names of various Indian tribes. But their work did not become widely disseminated. Escalante's diary manuscript was transmitted through channels to the Viceroy in Mexico and ultimately to the King of Spain. Miera drew several maps to illustrate their discoveries, but apparently none was ever printed. It remained for a German scientist, Humbolt, to make known to the world the achievements of the Domínguez-Escalante expedition.

Humbolt came to Spanish America is 1799 and stayed for five years, gathering material from which he wrote his *Political Essay on the Kingdom of New Spain.* The original edition was in French; an English edition in four volumes appeared in 1811. The *Essay,* accompanied by a large folio atlas, contains a detailed description of the northern frontier of New Spain based upon actual exploration. Humboldt himself never visited the northern regions, but he talked to those who had and he used the best manuscript and printed sources he could find. Apparently he did not find Escalante's diary, but from secondary sources he did bring Miera's geography into his own "Carte Générale."

Miera's multi-colored maps were beautifully done. The relief is shown in actual landforms: His mesas are flat topped and they look like mesas.

The route of the Domínguez-Escalante exploration is clearly shown: Every campsite is indicated by name. The boundaries of named Indian tribes are drawn, and the map provides an abundance of ethnological and historical information.

Place names abound. The Rio Colorado is prominent, but in its course through the canyon country it is named the Rio de las Zaguaganas after the Utes. Higher up it becomes the Rio de San Rafael. The Rio de Nuestra Señora de los Dolores is identical with the Dolores River, but the Rio de Nabajóo (Navajo) is now known as the San Juan. The Sierra de la Sal and the Sierra de Abajo are about in their proper places. Navajo Mountain is called El Cerro Azul.

Miera's maps are very accurate indeed, considering the complexity of the terrain and the information available to him, but he did make a few huge and important mistakes. He imagined that Utah Lake and the Great Salt Lake were one, which he called Laguna de los Timpanogos, and he assumed it must have a navigable outlet to the Pacific Ocean. Miera also depicted Rio San Buenaventura, now called Green River, as flowing west and emptying into Sevier Lake, which he named Laguna de Miera.

These mistakes are easy to explain. When the Spaniards reached the Uinta Basin, they encountered the Green River but did not follow its course. Nevertheless, they did not imagine that the river would break directly through the Tavaputs Plateau. Rather, they guessed it must flow west and later identified it with another river, the Sevier, which they later encountered on their southward trek from Utah Lake. The explorers heard of the Great Salt Lake, though they did not visit it. They could not conceive of a briny lake that did not have an outlet to the sea, and so Miera gave it one. The Spaniards, in their exploration from Utah Lake south beyond Sevier Lake, were actually traveling along the edge of the Great Basin, which has no outlet to the sea. But they did not know this. Instead, they thought of themselves as being on the western slope of the Rockies (known to the Spaniards as Sierra de las Grullas). Therefore, they thought that all the streams they saw must eventually reach the Pacific, including the Rio Timpanogos and the Rio San

Buenaventura, as well as the Colorado. Humbolt adopted this geography, and its implications, with little change.

These explorers were dreaming the dream of Columbus: They were looking for a shortcut to India. And Humbolt embellished this dream in his *Essay,* publishing eight small maps that indicated possible commercial routes across the North American continent. One showed a projected communication between the headwaters of the Rio Grande and those of the Colorado. He said that this route would not "be interesting for commerce, till great changes introduce colonization into their fertile and temperate regions." Observing the rapid westward advance of the Anglo-Americans, he concluded, "these changes are perhaps not very distant." Indeed they weren't.

After 1776, Spain became involved indirectly in the American Revolution and political complications in Europe followed. Thus, Spain sent no more official explorers to the canyon country. Soon, Spanish subjects of New Spain also revolted: Miguel Hidalgo y Costilla rang the liberty bell in 1810, and eleven years later Mexico emerged free and independent. Mexico inherited from Spain all of the country west of the Continental Divide and south of 42nd parallel of north latitude. Yet, during the next twenty-five years of Mexican control, few permanent settlements were established beyond the limits of the frontier set by Spain, and certainly none in the canyon country of the Colorado. During that time though, the course of the Green River was correctly charted and the imaginary Rio San Buenaventura disappeared.

CARAVANS AND FURS

There was little to attract New Mexicans to the canyon because few Indians lived there. Those who ventured there were primarily traders interested in establishing a more direct route to the Ute settlements on the eastern edge of the Great Basin. Many of these traders were slavers who exchanged guns, horses, and woolen blankets for Paiute women and children, whom they could then take back and sell as household servants in New Mexico.

It was surely they who worked out a good trail, which cut across the southwestern tip of Colorado,

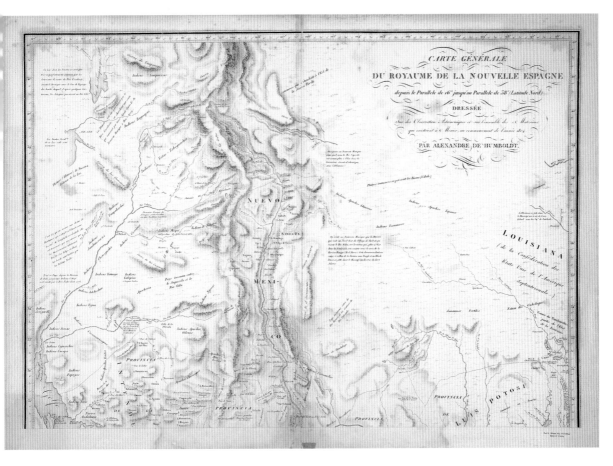

crossed the Colorado River near present-day Moab and the Green River below the Book Cliffs, and followed the cliffs northeast to the base of the Wasatch Plateau. Crossing the plateau by way of the Price River and Spanish Fork Canyon, travelers would arrive at Utah Lake.

From the Green River crossing, a southern branch of the trail arced around the northern end of the San Rafael Swell, traversed the Castle Valley, and crossed Wasatch Pass, followed Salina Canyon to the Sevier Valley. This southern branch continued southwest from the Sevier Valley and became known as the Spanish Trail, despite the fact that it was established in the Mexican epoch.

The Crossing of the Fathers route was also used to some extent during the Mexican era, although precious little documentation exists. One party that did take this route was a caravan led by New Mexican trader Antonio Armijo. His party crossed at the ford in December 1829. While making

improvements to the ford, they noted some inscriptions on the cliff wall, which they thought had been made by Domínguez and Escalante more than half a century earlier. It is doubtful that the Spanish friars took time to stop and doodle on the rocks. It is more likely that another party left their marks. In any event, the inscriptions have since disappeared beneath the waters of Lake Powell.

Armijo's trip marked the opening of the annual caravan trade between New Mexico and southern California, which lasted for two decades. The Crossing of the Fathers cutoff was not suitable for such heavy traffic and was probably not used very often. The Longer Spanish Trail was a less direct route, but it also was less arduous. Pack mules hauled woolens from New Mexico more than one thousand miles to the Pacific Coast, where the goods were exchanged for horses and mules. Sometimes more than one hundred traders would

form a caravan. On the return trip, traders would drive as many as a thousand animals.

While the Mexican traders were inclined to travel quickly through the canyon country, American fur trappers saw it as a destination. When Mexico gained its independence in 1821, Spanish colonial restrictions were lifted and trade commenced between the Missouri frontier and the United States and New Mexico over the Sante Fe Trail. Some Americans traveled with the caravans to California and even entered the trade, but more became involved in the fur trade.

American mountain men literally mapped the central Rocky Mountains on beaver skin. After 1821, trappers from Santa Fe and Taos ranged north and west into the upper basin of the Colorado River, and by 1824 they had reached the Green River in the Uinta Basin. This became an important base of operations. Beaver are plentiful in the canyon country even today, and must have been abundant during the great days of the fur trade, 1820–1840.

Antoine Roubidoux, one of the more prominent fur trade entrepreneurs in Utah, established a trading post at White Rocks in the Uinta Basin in 1831. His trappers traveled as far south as the Gila River in central Arizona in search of pelts. Denis Julien, who inscribed his name and the date

Horseshoe Bend on the Colorado River, Glen Canyon National Recreation Area, Arizona Jay Dusard

1831 near Roubidoux's post, later left his autograph at several locations in the canyon country. Marks bearing Julien's name an 1836 date have been found in Hell Roaring and Stillwater canyons on the Green River, and Cataract Canyon on the Colorado River. The Hell Roaring Canyon inscription includes what appears to be a boat traveling over whitewater rapids.

We know little more about Julien. He was quite probably a typical mountain man who would go anywhere to trap beaver. Julien's inscriptions are the earliest records we have of American presence in the deeper canyons, and strongly suggest that he may have been the first explorer to discover that the Green River flows into the Colorado. Unfortunately, neither Julien nor his contemporaries who trapped these canyons left written records of their experiences, and so the intimate geographic knowledge they acquired was mostly lost. But the major trails blazed by these trappers and traders would become the principal roads by which we access the canyon country today.

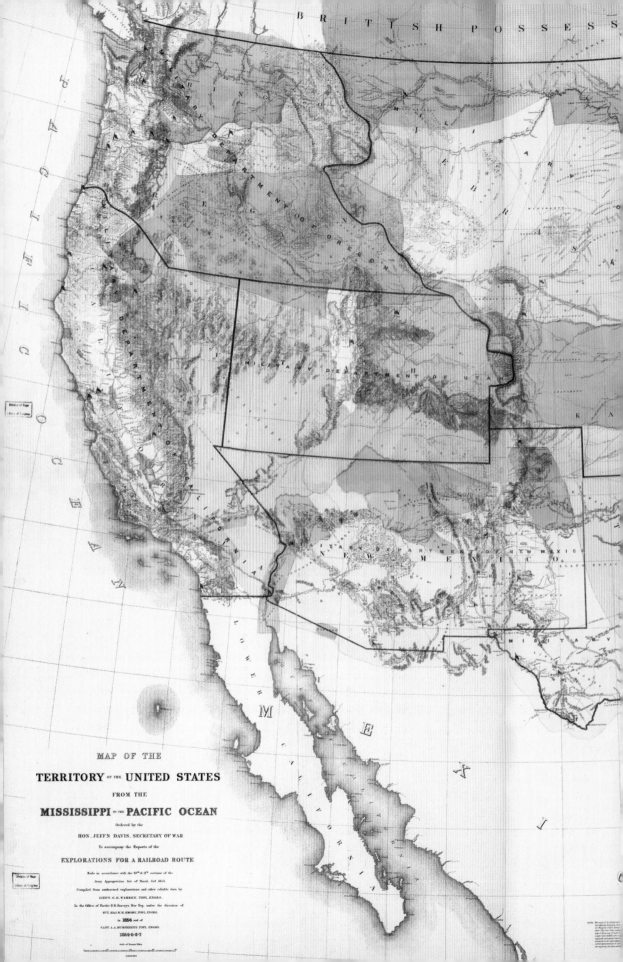

MAP OF THE

TERRITORY of the **UNITED STATES**

FROM THE

MISSISSIPPI to the **PACIFIC OCEAN**

Ordered by the

HON. JEFF'N DAVIS, SECRETARY OF WAR

To accompany the Reports of the

EXPLORATIONS FOR A RAILROAD ROUTE

3

TOPOGRAPHICAL ENGINEERS

THE ROAD TO CATHAY

ON MAY 23, 1844, John C. Frémont of the
U.S. Army's Corps of Topographical Engineers,
on the way home from his second expedition,
stopped at Utah Lake, where Domínguez and
Escalante had camped sixty-eight years earlier.
There he came to a reluctant conclusion.

On his way west, Frémont had followed the
Oregon Trail, but then turned south and crossed
the 42nd parallel—the Adam-Onis Treaty Line
marking the international boundary between
United States territory and Mexico. Frémont
ostensibly was searching for the river that was
believed to flow west from Laguna de los
Timpanogos to the Pacific, as first mapped by
Miera and elaborated upon by Humbolt and
others. He crossed the Sierra Nevada, explored
the Central Valley of California, and then
returned over the Spanish Trail to Utah Lake.

Frémont's trek officially confirmed what the
fur men had known for some time: The country
between the Wasatch Mountains and the Sierra
Nevada was a great basin with no outlet to the sea,
and he so named it. He also renamed the Great
Basin's principal westbound stream the Humbolt
River, thereby honoring the spirit, if not the
accuracy, of the legendary German cartographer.

Frémont demolished one of the most influential
myths in North American exploration. Since 1776,
Miera's Rio San Buenaventura and the outlet from
Laguna de los Timpanogos to the sea had been
accepted without question, and often embellished,

East Moody Wash, Glen Canyon National Recreation Area, Utah STU LEVY

by imaginative cartographers. These fictitious rivers of the West had interested generations of explorers, including Meriwether Lewis and William Clark, Zebulon Pike, various voyagers coasting Pacific shores, the Hudson's Bay Company, and American fur men.

Frémont's great maps of the West, drawn by Charles Preuss and published in 1845 and 1848, outlined the Great Basin and disposed of the mythical rivers. On the first map, the canyon country of the Colorado River is blank. On the second map, the Green and the Grand (Colorado) are located, although the mouth of the Green is too far south. In contrast to the commercial map publishers, the Topographical Engineers, in mapping the new western lands of the United States, exhibited admirable restraint. As a rule, areas not known to them were left blank or labeled "unexplored."

"Hypothetical geography," said William H. Emory of the Engineers, "has proceeded far enough in the United States." For some three decades after Frémont's maps were published, updated maps produced by the Topographical Engineers and other government-sponsored expeditions continued to label the canyon country generally as "unexplored."

The ink had hardly dried on Frémont's 1845 map when the United States declared war on Mexico. Gen. Stephen Watts Kearny marched into Santa Fe in August 1846, and the vanguard of Mormon pioneers led by Brigham Young arrived on the shores of the Great Salt Lake the following summer. Hostilities with Mexico formally ceased with the signing of the Treaty of Guadalupe Hidalgo in February 1848, whereby Mexico ceded to the United States nearly half of its territory, including all lands north of the Gila River.

That same year, gold was discovered in California, which triggered a great migration westward that was to continue unabated for the next decade. As Humbolt had predicted, great changes were indeed taking place in the West.

The bright lure of golden California prompted travelers to search for the most suitable routes across the continent. During the Gold Rush, the Spanish Trail through the canyon country was little used. Why bother with such a long, winding trail through rough country when you could take the shorter, southern routes opened during the war with Mexico, or the more central Oregon Trail and its Humbolt River cutoff to California?

Much more attention was given to the canyon country during the search for a route for the first transcontinental railroad. Everyone agreed the line would have to be built, but where? Sectional rivalry between the northern and southern states delayed the decision. There also was uncertainty about some of the blank places on the map. So, in 1853, Congress authorized the War Department to find the best route, and secretary of war Jefferson Davis directed the Corps of Topographical Engineers to survey four routes.

Having given up the idea of a river route to the Pacific, Frémont and his influential father-in-law, Missouri Senator Thomas Hart Benton, got behind the railroads. They backed a central route in the expectation that its terminus would be St. Louis. Senator Benton tried to have Frémont appointed to head the official 1853 survey of the central route, but the command fell to Lt. John W. Gunnison. Undeterred, the senator enlisted private interests to underwrite an independent expedition for his son-in-law, and persuaded

E.F. Beale to popularize the central route by traveling overland from St. Louis to his new post as superintendent of Indian Affairs in California.

Beale got underway first, followed by Gunnison and the official railroad surveyors. Frémont brought up the rear. All of these parties came into the canyon country from Colorado across the open lands at the foot of the Book Cliffs. They all crossed the Green River at the crossing long used by traders on the Spanish Trail. They all continued along the established, well-worn trail through Castle Valley. Beale and Gunnison then left the canyon country through Wasatch Pass and Salina Canyon while Frémont went south to the head of the Fremont River and reached the Sevier after crossing the Awapa Plateau.

The northern edge of the canyon country thus came prominently into public view as a result of these explorations. In 1854, Gwinn Harris Heap, who had traveled with Beale, published *A Central*

Snow patterns on San Rafael Swell near Factory Butte, Utah   Tom Till

Route to the Pacific, with an accompanying map. The most informative and detailed description of the country traversed was that written by Lt. E.G. Beckwith for the Gunnison survey. Frémont also wrote a letter published in a Washington newspaper, in which he said, "Europe still lies between Asia and America. Build this railroad and things will have revolved about: America will lie between Asia and Europe—the golden vein which runs through the history of the world will follow the iron track to San Francisco…"

On May 10, 1869, at Promontory Point north of the Great Salt Lake, the last spike connected the rails and the dream of a western road to Cathay was realized. One line was scarcely enough to serve the needs of a rapidly expanding West, however, and within fourteen years the Denver & Rio Grande Western Railroad bridged the Green River at the old Spanish Trail.

American explorers also approached the periphery of canyon country from the south, as well, in the first decade after the Mexican War. In 1849, Lt. James H. Simpson joined Lt. Col. John M. Washington's command for a punitive raid into the Navajo country. Heading west from Santa Fe, they encountered the vast, prehistoric

ruins of Chaco Canyon and Canyon de Chelly, and returned by way of Zuni and El Morro, also known as Inscription Rock. Among other things, Simpson gleaned enough information to hint broadly in his report that the valley of the Colorado River might be passable.

Shades of Alexander von Humbolt! Communication between the oceans by way of the Rio Grande and the Rio Colorado might be possible. Everyone knew the Colorado reached the Pacific by way of the Gulf of California. But did it really flow through a canyon? The Santa Fe traders told Simpson it did, but he was not convinced.

In 1851, Capt. Lorenzo Sitgreaves of the Topographical Engineers was dispatched to settle the matter. He was instructed to explore the Zuni River to its mouth and then follow the Colorado to the Gulf of California. Sitgreaves found that the Zuni discharged into the Little Colorado, which he then followed until it began to drop into a canyon. Unable to proceed further, he headed west and encountered the Colorado when he reached the Mojave villages. Two years later, Lt. A.M. Whipple—closely paralleling Sitgreaves' trail—surveyed a route for one of the four transcontinental railroad routes under consideration.

Flat Top Rock, Grand Staircase-Escalante National Monument, Utah John P. George

Ponderosa pine and aspen on Boulder Mountain, Dixie National Forest, Utah Scott T. Smith

The tracks of the Atlantic and Pacific Railroad, which would become the Santa Fe Railway, followed.

Gunnison's survey had cut across the northern edge of the canyon country, and Whipple had skirted it on the south. In 1857, Lt. G.K. Warren, topographical engineer, published his great "Map of the Territory of the United States from the Mississippi to the Pacific Ocean" which incorporated all the works of the Pacific railroad surveys and many other sources. On this exhaustively detailed map, the canyon country remained a featureless blank space marked "unexplored."

A LAND OF WONDER

If relations between the United States government and the Mormons of Utah had not degenerated into open hostility in 1857–58, the Topographical Engineers might have ended their explorations in and near the canyon country with the railroad surveys. President James Buchanan ordered a force of twenty-five hundred troops under the command of Albert S. Johnston to enforce the authority of the new federal governor appointed to replace Brigham Young. Fearful that the "invasion" would open the gates to the mob violence that the Mormons had fled to Utah to escape, Young took up the gauntlet. The Mormons employed guerrilla tactics to slow down Johnston's advancing army. The federal troops were forced to spend a cold winter near Fort Bridger. In the spring of 1858, relations thawed, the parties negotiated a truce, and federal troops entered Salt Lake City. Eventually, the Army established a permanent presence at Camp Floyd, forty miles outside the city.

The success of Mormon guerrilla warfare in the opening days of the war, and the logistical isolation of the military forces, caused the War Department to seek new supply routes to Utah. In 1859, Washington directed the Corps of Topographical Engineers to conduct a number of expeditions that would supplement the work of the railroad surveys and increase geographic knowledge of the various approaches to Utah. Capt. James H. Simpson, who as a lieutenant a decade earlier had probed the heart of Navajo country, found a new wagon road across the Great Basin and provided a more detailed description of the basin than had Frémont. His report also carried a map of the Domínguez-Escalante route plotted from their diary by Philip Harry. The year before, Lt. Joseph C. Ives steamed up the lower Colorado in the U.S.S. Explorer and found it navigable as far as Black Canyon, where Hoover Dam now stands.

Also in 1859, Capt. John N. Macomb was ordered to take an expedition directly into the canyon country. He was to determine the course of the San Juan River, to fix the position of the confluence of the Green and Grand, or Colorado, rivers, and to find the best and most direct route between the Rio Grande and the southern settlements of Utah. The canyon country was still something of a mystery. The most up-to-date map, published by the Topographical Engineers in 1858, noted, "Region Unexplored Scientifically."

Dr. John Strong Newberry
UNIVERSITY OF UTAH

Macomb worked in the field from mid-July to the end of September 1859. His party included Dr. John Strong Newberry, who had served as geologist with the Ives expedition the year before. The team followed the well-defined Spanish Trail past Mesa Verde, across the Sage Plain to the Ojo Verde, a spring midway between the La Sal and Abajo mountains. There they established a base camp and Macomb, Newberry, and a few others headed west to find the confluence of the Green and the Grand. They traveled about thirty miles, probably down Indian Creek, judging by Newberry's description. Following this stream, they soon found themselves in a canyon. Unable to reach the river, they climbed out to the rim and found a high point where they could see the Colorado. The explorers were able to satisfy themselves that they were only a short distance from the confluence. Newberry, in particular, was highly impressed by the view of what came to be called The Needles.

"Toward the west the view reached some thirty miles, there bounded by long lines and bold angles of mesa walls similar to those behind us, while in the intervening space the surface was diversified by columns, spires, castles, and battlemented towers of colossal but often beautiful proportions, closely resembling elaborate structures of art, but in effect far surpassing the most imposing monuments of human skill. In the southwest was a longer line of spires of white stones standing on red bases, thousands in number, but so slender as to recall the most delicate carving in ivory or the fairy architecture of some Gothic cathedral; yet many, perhaps most, were over five hundred feet in height, and thickly set in a narrow belt or series of some miles in length. The appearance was so strange and beautiful as to call out exclamations of delight from all our party."

Bearing in mind the objective of the exploration, Macomb wrote: "I cannot conceive of a more worthless and impracticable region than the one we now find ourselves in. I doubt not that there are repetitions and varieties of it for hundreds of miles down the cañon of the Great Colorado, for I have heard of but one crossing of that river above the vicinity of the Mojave Village, and I have reason to doubt if that one is practicable, except with utmost care, even for a pack-mule."

Unable to reach the San Juan by following the Colorado, the full expedition turned south from Ojo Verde to find their objective. From one elevated point, a short distance south of the present town of Blanding, Newberry tells us the explorers obtained a beautiful view of the country bordering the San Juan. This included Mesa Verde, Shiprock, the Carrizo Mountains, Monument Valley, and the Bear's Ears.

Newberry was particularly impressed by what would later be called Monument Valley, visible more than thirty-five miles away and framed by a great gap "through which the San Juan flows to its junction with the Colorado.

Grand Canyon National Park, Arizona Huntington Witherill

"The features presented by this remarkable gate-way are among the most striking and impressive of any included in the scenery of the Colorado country," Newberry wrote. "The distance between the mesa walls on the north and south is perhaps ten miles, and scattered over the interval are many castle-like buttes and slender towers, none of which can be less than one thousand feet in height, their sides absolutely perpendicular, their forms wonderful imitations of the structures of human art. Illuminated by the setting sun, the outlines of these singular objects came out sharp and distinct, with such exact similitude of art, and contrast with nature as usually displayed that we could hardly resist the conviction that we beheld the walls and towers of some Cyclopean city hitherto undiscovered in this far-off region. Within the great area enclosed by the grander features I have enumerated, the

country is set with numberless buttes and isolated mesas, which give to the scene in a high degree the peculiar character I have so often referred to as exhibited by the eroded districts of the great central plateau. Here and there we caught glimpses of the vivid green of the wooded bottomlands of the river, generally concealed by the intermediate and overhanging cliffs."

Having seen from this elevated position how rough the canyon country to the west was, they realized that they could not travel to the mouth of the San Juan. Therefore, Macomb continued directly south to the river, probably reaching it in the vicinity of present-day Bluff. The expedition then turned upstream and returned to Santa Fe by way of the Cañon Largo tributary and Jemez Pueblo.

Macomb had demonstrated to his own satisfaction, at least, that there was no suitable supply route through to settlements in southern Utah. Communication would have to follow existing trails, and of these the Crossing of the Fathers was scarcely one practical for military purposes. Apart from the immediate objective of the expedition, however, Newberry's descriptions of the country they traversed were highly valuable and his geological report was the first to shed light on the eastern side of the canyon country. The location of the confluence of the Green and the Grand, or Colorado, rivers, as well as the course of the San Juan River above the canyon, were accurately determined. So were the La Sal and Abajo mountains and the Bear's Ears, among other landmarks.

The discoveries of the Macomb expedition were first published in a map of the territory and military department of Utah, in 1860. This map accurately depicts a single Spanish Trail, rather than the two routes that were more speculatively defined on the 1854 Gunnison map. The Domínguez-Escalante route, plotted by Philip Harry and later published in Simpson's 1876 *Report of Explorations Across the Great Basin,* also appears on this map.

The Macomb material was later included, in greater detail and on a larger scale, on the official map of the expedition, made by F.W. Egloffstein and included in the final report, which was not published until 1876. Both Newberry and Egloffstein also had accompanied Ives, and the reports of the Ives and Macomb expeditions should be regarded as complementary.

Egloffstein invented a new technique that delicately illustrated the sculptured land. His beautiful maps portray the Colorado River canyon country from the Book Cliffs to a point far below the "Big Cañon," or Grand Canyon. These maps very nicely summarize the accomplishments of the Corps of Topographical Engineers beginning in 1848, when Frémont published his map of the West. The true course of the Colorado River is plotted, and geographical fictions have largely disappeared. The canyon country itself is still largely blank, but Egloffstein's map omits the phrase "Region Unexplored Scientifically." As a result of Newberry's pioneering geological studies and the exploratory work of the Topographical Engineers, those who followed would be much less concerned with finding a viable route through the canyons and much more interested in the country itself.

4

THE SCIENTISTS

THE MAN WITH ONE ARM

MAJ. JOHN WESLEY POWELL served in the Union Army during the Civil War and lost his right forearm at the battle of Shiloh. Undismayed by this disability, and consumed by an interest in science and a love of adventure, Powell spent much of 1867 and 1868 exploring the Rocky Mountains of Colorado. While in the field, he developed a great interest in the Colorado River. Several explorers had crossed it, but rumors of canyons, whirlpools, and waterfalls persisted and no one had yet tried to navigate the river for any great distance. Powell was determined to mount an expedition that would be the first to do so.

On May 24, 1869, only two weeks after the last spike was driven to link the Union Pacific and Central Pacific railroads at Promontory Point, Powell and nine companions in four boats embarked from the Union Pacific's Green River crossing in Wyoming, elevation sixty-one hundred feet. By July 13, they had successfully navigated the canyons of the Uinta Range and the Tavaputs Plateau and had reached the Green River crossing of the Spanish Trail, elevation 4,064 feet.

Keeping on, they glided past the mouth of the San Rafael River, wound through Labyrinth Canyon, and then entered Stillwater Canyon, where the current quieted "as if in no haste to leave this beautiful canyon," Powell wrote. The canyon walls grew progressively higher until they were twelve hundred feet above river level, and the explorers had reached the junction of the Green

Maj. John Wesley Powell with Paiute chief Tau-Gu
JOHN K. HILLERS

Glen Canyon as seen by Maj. John Wesley Powell's 1871-72 survey party (stereoscopic image)
James Fennemore

and Grand, or Colorado, rivers. There, the elevation at the water's edge was 3,875 feet.

Powell's party spent the next few days at this junction, while he and George Y. Bradley climbed out on the east side of the canyon. "The scenery from the top is the same old picture of desolation we have seen for the last hundred miles. Curiously shaped spires and domes rise everywhere…," Bradley observed in his diary, becoming the second person to record his impressions of The Needles. Ten years earlier, Macomb and Newberry had seen this same landscape from a point about fifteen miles to the east, and decided to turn back.

Powell and his party pressed on. The morning of July 21 they shoved off into the Colorado River and soon encountered fast water in Cataract Canyon, a name Powell put on the map. For twelve days they toiled, portaging and lining, while running the forty-mile-long succession of rapids.

"Sometimes the waves below would roll over a boat…Now and then the boat would roll over; but clinging to its sides until they could right it, the men would swim to shore, towing it with them. We found much difficulty in the whirlpools below; for at times it was almost impossible to get out of them. They would carry us back under the falls, they would dash us against the rocks, or they would send us swirling down the river," Powell wrote. Finally, on July 28, they came out on smooth water at the river's confluence with a muddy stream that they named the Dirty Devil. The elevation at that point was 3,460 feet.

From this point, it was easy going for a few days. The men rested on their oars and enjoyed the scenery. After the rough and ragged walls of Cataract, Powell was much impressed by the "mounds and cones and hills of solid sandstone, rising one above the other as they stretched back in a gentle slope for miles," and he initially named this placid stretch Mound Canyon. Beyond the confluence with the San Juan River, the landscape changed again.

"We had now run once more into dark red and chocolate-coloured sandstones, with slate-coloured beds below: these usually form vertical walls, occasionally terraced or broken down, and from the crest of these, the orange mounds sloped back, bearing on top of each mound some variegated monument, now vertical, now terraced, now carved by time into grotesque shapes, such as towers, pinnacles, etc. These monuments stood alone or in groups, and spread over the landscape as far as the eye could reach…We named it Monument Canyon."

On August 1 and 2, 1869, the explorers camped just beyond the mouth of the San Juan River. Here, near the entrance to a short, narrow canyon, they discovered a spectacular, grotto-like chamber arched over by high, vaulting walls. The singing wind and the unusual acoustical properties of the chamber suggested the name Music Temple. While Powell was making observations nearby, three of the men—O.G. Howland, Seneca Howland, and William Dunn—carved their names on the rock wall of the chamber. After his work was done on August 2, Powell himself took a long nap in the Music Temple, an act repeated by many river travelers until 1963, when the rising waters of the reservoir drowned the grotto. Powell recalled these cool, shady side canyons when he later coined the name Glen Canyon to describe the entire, magnificent stretch between the Dirty Devil and Paria rivers. On

August 4, after passing the Crossing of the Fathers, the explorers reached the mouth of the Paria River, elevation 3,120 feet.

The Powell expedition would spend twenty-six more days braving the white water of Marble Canyon and the Grand Canyon before arriving in open country at the mouth of the Virgin River, at 750 feet. Of the ten men who embarked from the Green River crossing in Wyoming, six completed the journey. One left the expedition at the Uinta River. O.G. Howland, Seneca Howland, and William Dunn—the same trio who had inscribed their names at Music Temple—quit the expedition just when victory was in sight. The men preferred to climb out of the Grand Canyon at Separation Canyon rather than risk their lives running one more set of rapids. But Shivwitz warriors killed all three men before they could reach the nearest Mormon settlement.

Powell's 1869 expedition was without precedent. He and his men successfully negotiated one thousand miles of the canyons of the Colorado. At several points along the way, Powell climbed

Paria Canyon-Vermilion Cliffs Wilderness, Arizona STU LEVY

out to the rims to study the surrounding country. He collected plants, made geological sections, and observed the stars at night. He studied Ancestral Pueblo ruins. He put names on the map. He appreciated the beauty and grandeur of the landscape all the way.

"Here ended the 'Great Unknown,'" Powell said as the trip ended. Clearly, the Colorado was not a commercially viable route to the Pacific.

"Before we started I was called a damned fool for embarking in such an enterprise, for nobody possibly gets through," wrote Jack Sumner, a member of Powell's party. "Since I have got through, I have been called a damned fool for the same thing, because there has been many men long since that have proved that there was nothing to go for as they have it all." But, unlike the stay-at-homes, Jack had seen the elephant. "If anybody disbelieves any of this, or wants to know more of the cañons of the Colorado, go and see it," he said.

In 1871–72, Powell mounted a broader geographical and scientific examination of the vast plateau and canyons of the Colorado with funds appropriated by Congress and under the auspices of the Smithsonian Institution. This expedition, which was better organized for the collection of information and less adventurous, was patterned after those being conducted elsewhere in the West by colleagues such as Ferdinand V. Hayden and George M. Wheeler.

On May 22, Powell and his ten-man crew left Green River, Wyoming, in three boats. They reached the Green River Crossing in Utah on August 26, spent ten days in Cataract Canyon, and arrived at the Dirty Devil River on September 30. A week later, they reached the Crossing of the Fathers, where they picked up supplies that Jacob Hamblin, a Mormon scout, had left for them. They then floated down to the mouth of the Paria River, where they concluded their river exploration for the year.

Powell's team spent the winter surveying and mapping the canyon country of southern Utah and the Arizona Strip. In August, they resumed the river trip, going as far as Kanab Canyon, where they abandoned their boats and walked out.

The report Powell ultimately produced in 1874 was a composite account that incorporated data accumulated on both trips. It makes no mention of the 1871–72 exploration, per se. To Powell, the 1869 expedition must have been the most important. On that trip he and his companions had conquered the unknown and accomplished what no one had done before. The second voyage largely duplicated the first, but allowed more time for Powell and his team to observe and collect.

Member of 1871-72 Powell Survey at the rim of the Grand Canyon
JOHN K. HILLERS

The ideas and concepts Powell developed on his voyages found expression later in works of high value in geology, ethnology, land classification, and reclamation. His report contained a broad analysis of the process and results of land sculpture as revealed in the Colorado Plateau. It is regarded as a basic work in regional geological literature.

In his own studies, Powell found numerous gaps in geological knowledge. He directed his appointees to fill them. Capt. Clarence E. Dutton studied and identified the High Plateaus before

Maj. John Wesley Powell's armchair-equipped boat used during his 1871-72 survey of the plateau and canyons of the Colorado River (stereoscopic image) JOHN K. HILLERS

going on to the study of the Grand Canyon. Dutton found the canyon country highly appealing and his vivid, dramatic prose reflects this. His literary style is of a caliber seldom found in geological literature. Grove K. Gilbert contributed a celebrated report on the Henry Mountains, which Powell named for Smithsonian Institution Secretary Joseph Henry.

Drawings by prominent artists such as William Henry Holmes and Thomas Moran, and photographs by E.O. Beaman, James Fennemore, and John K. Hillers, illustrated the Powell Survey volumes. A.H. Thompson and his associates made the first satisfactory maps of the canyon country, incorporating important discoveries made during their own reconnaissance. For example, Thompson differentiated the drainages of the Paria, Escalante, and Dirty Devil rivers. He also sketched out the main features of the Aquarius and Kaiparowits plateaus, the Waterpocket Fold, and the Henry Mountains. His geographic contour maps provided the base on which Powell, Dutton, and Gilbert recorded their geological findings.

By 1880, all the reports were published: Powell on the river explorations and the physical structure of the Colorado Basin (1876), the Uinta Mountains (1876), and the arid lands of the United States with particular reference to Utah (1879); Gilbert on the Henry Mountains (1877); and Dutton on the High Plateaus (1880).

WHEELER AND HAYDEN

The Wheeler Survey, officially called the United States Geographical Surveys West of the One Hundredth Meridian, was designed to examine, describe, and map the resources of the West. In 1869 and 1871, while reconnoitering through Nevada and Arizona, George M. Wheeler became enamored with the Colorado River and seems to have tried to vie with Powell in the scientific conquest of the plateau and canyon country.

Wheeler headed a team from the Army Corps of Engineers, which merged with the Corps of Topographical Engineers during the Civil War. His staff of officers, engineers, and scientists mapped the region northward from the Grand Canyon to the High Plateaus, and from Nevada eastward to the Crossing of the Fathers in Glen Canyon. His reconnaissance parties crossed the trail of Powell's men on the Dirty Devil, Escalante,

Great Gallery of Fremont culture pictographs in Horseshoe Canyon, Canyonlands National Park, Utah LINDA CONNOR

and Paria rivers, at Lee's Ferry, and elsewhere. Edwin E. Howell and Grove K. Gilbert first served with Wheeler in 1869 before joining Powell's 1871 survey.

Although Wheeler's men explored and mapped portions of the canyon country during the course of their explorations, most of their publications did not touch the canyon country. Wheeler's final *Report* (1889) summarizes the entire work of his survey and the impressive volumes on geology, botany, zoology, and archeology are basic reference works. One of the enduring contributions made by the Wheeler Survey was the excellent atlas of hachured and shaded maps, two of which—sheets 59 and 67—cover the region from the High Plateaus to the Grand Canyon.

While Powell and Wheeler were zealously studying the west side of the canyon country, Ferdinand V. Hayden was busy surveying Colorado and an adjoining strip of Utah extending approximately to the longitude of Bluff and Moab and including the Four Corners region in the San Juan Valley. Hayden's team included notables such as W.H. Holmes, A.C. Peale, Henry Gannett, G.B. Chittenden, and W.H. Jackson. In 1874–75, the Hayden party explored, mapped, and studied topography, geology, and archeology, carrying on where Macomb and Newberry had left off.

The La Sal, Abajo, and Carrizo mountains, and Ute Mountain, received particular attention. Holmes anticipated Gilbert in formulating the hypothesis of laccolithic origins of mountains, a fact recognized by Gilbert, who named one of the peaks in the Henry Mountains after Holmes. Jackson and Holmes described their discoveries of prehistoric ruins in Mesa Verde, Hovenweep, and elsewhere in the Four Corners region. Jackson took the first photographs of these important sites, and Holmes made sketches and drawings of them.

The reports of these investigations are found in the annual publications and bulletins emanating from the Hayden Survey. Although these works

William Henry Holmes
UNIVERSITY OF UTAH

cannot be compared with the artistic productions of the Powell Survey, they do contain information of basic scientific value on the eastern side of canyon country. Hayden also produced a topographic contour map of Colorado. Extending into Utah and Arizona, it equaled the maps published by Powell and Wheeler.

By 1880, as a result of concerted study by the Powell, Wheeler, and Hayden expeditions, the world could see the canyon country in broad outline and intimate detail. Only the San Juan Triangle and the Navajo country west of Monument Valley and Marsh Pass were not covered by any of the three great public surveys.

Powell, Wheeler, and Hayden showed how climate, topography, and the behavior of streams impose controls on vegetation, and these conditions could serve as guides to economic development. In the absence of minerals other than coal, they concluded that the region would be suitable primarily for grazing. Farming the limited agricultural land was practicable only under irrigation. In *Arid Lands* (1879), Powell and A.H. Thompson delineated the irrigable lands along the Paria, Escalante, San Rafael, and other streams of the Colorado Basin, most of which already were occupied by Mormons. Thompson's accompanying map of Utah was the first really accurate map of the territory.

When the Great Surveys were consolidated to form the U.S. Geological Survey in 1879, Clarence King was appointed the first director and Powell was assigned to the Smithsonian Institution to continue the anthropological investigations he had begun as a part of his survey. In 1879, he became the first director of the Smithsonian's Bureau of American Ethnology, a post he held to the end of his life. In 1881, when King resigned from the Geological Survey, Powell was appointed to the directorship of that agency, as well, a post he occupied until 1894.

5

CANYON COUNTRY PRIMEVAL

THE CONDITIONS OF LIFE

VERY SOON AFTER THEIR ARRIVAL in the valley of the Great Salt Lake in 1847, the Latter-day Saints began exploring the mountainous terrain east and west, north and south, looking for habitable, arable land in the river valleys and appraising the resources of the desert lands. Within ten years, dozens of frontier settlements had been established hundreds of miles from Salt Lake City.

Mormon pioneers easily and naturally followed the Spanish Trail. In June 1855, Alfred N. Billings and a company of forty-one men established the first canyon country settlement, Elk Mountain Mission, at the Colorado River crossing where Moab is now located. They brought with them sixteen oxen-drawn wagons loaded with flour, wheat, corn, potatoes, peas, oats, and hardware such as whipsaws, axes, scythes, iron bars, trowels, hoes, shovels, and plows. They also drove a herd of dairy cattle and horses.

The Billings party left the Great Basin by way of Salina Canyon and traveled the Spanish Trail through Castle Valley to the Green River. From there, they crossed the dry desert between the Green and the Colorado rivers and, after considerable difficulty with the wagons in lower Moab Canyon, finally reached the Colorado and ferried across. They immediately began to build a fort, plant crops, dig irrigation ditches, and preach to the Utes.

John McEwan wrote to his brother, describing life in the frontier community. There was no

White Rim from Grand View Point, Canyonlands National Park, Utah GEORGE H.H. HUEY

45

timber, even firewood was scarce, and the land was sandy. McEwan's appreciation for the landscape seemed limited to the quality of the soil, or the lack thereof.

"How this soil will produce, I do not know; there is not much land for farming purposes anyhow. It is thick with sagebrush and greasewood, and nearly all sand....The Indians call this nothing but a kanyon. It is about three miles wide, mountains high and almost perpendicular where we are, of a reddish cast," he wrote.

"I have suffered more than I can express at present for want of water to drink," he added. "The sun's piercing rays and the sun burning your feet under you, soon dries a man up. I have been sick after being alkalied. I am just getting over it."

Much less rain falls west of the 100th meridian than east of it. Twenty inches of annual precipitation or less is the rule in most areas, but the canyon country of southeastern Utah and northeastern Arizona receives only half that amount. The West in general is semi-arid and dry. The canyon

country is arid and drier. But such overly general statements about the climate can be deceptive. Variations in weather from place to place are so pronounced that it is more accurate to say there are several local climates rather than one.

The highest altitudes receive the greatest amounts of rainfall, while the lowlands and the canyons get less. During the summer, brief afternoon thunderstorms and cloudbursts occur frequently and are usually widely scattered. When a heavy rain falls on slick-rock areas, it quickly runs off. Water collects in courses, roars down steep slopes, falls over canyon rims, and fills usually dry washes, which roil with mud, stones, and debris. Within a few hours after a storm passes, the bare rock surfaces will dry again, except for those occasional depressions where water collects. By morning, in the washes, only damp sand and a few shallow pools will remain from the deluge of the day before.

The lower levels of the canyon country, below sixty-five hundred feet, are poorly supplied with

Indian Creek Valley, Utah JAY DUSARD

water. Annual precipitation seldom reaches ten inches and in most places is about half that. The few perennial tributaries of the Green, Colorado, and San Juan rivers are fed mainly by snowmelt from the High Plateaus, the La Sal and Abajo mountains, and Elk Ridge. During spring runoff, the Paria, Escalante, Dirty Devil, and San Rafael rivers carry a considerable volume of water, but during the remainder of the year flows are greatly reduced and further diverted by irrigation. Small, spring-fed streams are common in the lower courses of the larger canyons that feed into the Green, Colorado, and San Juan rivers. Life in the canyon country is supported to a far greater extent by waters tributary to these rivers than by the master streams.

As one might expect, the lowest elevations have the warmest weather, although not all places at the same altitude experience the same temperature. Temperatures in any given locality will vary widely throughout the year, soaring to 110 degrees in summer and plunging to 10 degrees or more

below zero in winter. In summer, the difference between the daytime high and overnight low temperatures can be 50 degrees or more, and nights at the higher elevations can be uncomfortably cold.

Despite these extremes in temperature, the climate of the canyon country is healthful and invigorating. Skies are generally clear, prolonged periods of overcast are rare, and severe storms are infrequent. To escape the from the midday heat of spring and summer, one need only retreat to the shade of a rock outcrop or tree. On the open, treeless parts of their reservation, the Navajos beat the heat by erecting simple summer ramadas.

Vegetation is diverse but sparse in the arid lands of the canyon country. Dark green conifer forests of Douglas fir, spruce, and fir, interspersed with aspen, crown the highest elevations, above 8,000 feet. Between 6,500 and 8,000 feet, Ponderosa pine and Gambel Oak trees predominate. Low-lying pinyon, juniper, and sagebrush take over the terrain between 5,000 and 6,500 feet. Scrubby plants such as shadscale and blackbrush,

along with several cacti species, characterize the deserts below 4,500 feet. Grass grows at all elevations, but only at the highest levels does it carpet the soil. Water-loving cottonwood trees are common along the perennial streams, the wet floors of the deeper canyons, and springs. Deep in the Green and Colorado river canyons, willow trees compete with the cottonwoods for space along the riverbanks.

The relative sparseness of vegetation permits uninterrupted vistas over great distances, even on level terrain. At many points on the rims, at the breaks, and on the crests of folds and reefs, your eyes can travel quickly through three life zones. High landmarks may be seen from great distances and from many different points. Once you become familiar with the canyon country, you will seldom feel lost.

Many species of animals live in the canyon country. Mule deer graze the highlands in summer and drift down to the pinyon-juniper belt in winter. The inquisitive antelope favor life in the more open, lower country, while elusive bighorn sheep prefer the rougher rimrock overlooking the canyons. In the deserts, lizards skitter about, snakes slither among the rocks, and bats and rodents prowl at night.

Beaver are common along the Colorado and Green rivers, as well as in the cold streams formed by melting snows in the tall conifer forests. Larger species of fish are limited to the master streams and to a few of the perennial tributaries, like the Fremont and San Rafael rivers, where trout are caught near the headwaters. Carnivorous coyotes, foxes, skunks, and badgers range widely in the canyon country. Birds, including raptors such as eagles and hawks, soar overhead.

Most of the soil suitable for agriculture has been formed by stream action. It is likely to be loose in character, often shallow, but quite fertile in some areas. The alluvium-floored upper valleys of the perennial streams heading on the High Plateaus on the western side of the canyon country are extensive enough to support a number of towns and settlements. In the deep canyons at the lowest levels, the limited soil is particularly unstable. Marginal areas where prehistoric farmers once eked out a living have suffered from erosion.

Between the watercourses, soil consists of eroded material filling spaces between projecting rocks, or it appears as the soft surface of the disintegrating formation, such as the extensive shale soils found in Castle Valley and at the base of the Book Cliffs from Price to Grand Junction. There are only a few areas of extensive open land and these, like the Green River Desert and the Kaibito Plateau, may be loose and sandy. Many areas consist of bare rock and have no soil covering at all.

In a land of little rain, people live where irrigation stretches the annual flow of water. For human settlement, the best lands in the canyon country were around the edges, at the base of the High Plateaus and the Book Cliffs, at the foot of the La Sal and Abajo mountains, and Navajo Mountain. Water was not far away. Streams fed by melting snow attracted big game animals, provided ample water for livestock, and could be diverted for irrigation.

THE ANCIENT ONES

The Mormons of the Elk Mountain Mission were the first Euro-Americans to put the arable resources of the canyon country to the test. But they weren't the first farmers to have settled in the area.

In 1854, Brigham Young directed W.D. Huntington to lead an expedition to establish contact with the Navajos and to explore the southeastern part of the canyon country by way of the Spanish Trail. En route, the party explored a section along the San Juan River about fifty miles long and twenty-five miles wide and encountered many abandoned dwellings.

"The walls of many buildings are still standing entire," Huntington wrote. "…some of them three or four stories high, with the ends of the red cedar joists set in the wall, some projecting eight or ten inches, but worn to a point at their extremities…the first ruins we discovered were three stone buildings, crumbled to mere heaps. One appeared to have been a pottery, for in and around it were loads of fragments of crockery of fine quality, ornamented with a great variety of figures painted with various colors as bright as if put on but yesterday…

"From here we traveled ten miles, with occasional ruins by the way, and entered a deep kanyon with projecting shelves of rock and under those shelves were numerous houses or fortifications. The one we examined was divided into twenty-four rooms, each nearly square and enclosing an area of about 144 square feet. The front wall was built up to the overhanging cliff, which formed the roof, and was curved, and full or portholes. The stones were all squared and faced, were of an equal thickness, and laid up with joints broken in a workman-like manner," Huntington reported.

Three or four miles up the canyon from where Huntington and his party saw these remains, "buildings were everywhere in view, of various forms and dimensions, and in almost every stage of decay." After traveling twelve miles northeast of the San Juan River, they came to the head of a canyon, "whose sides or banks, even to the very head, were perpendicular, and shelving, and near the banks there was no soil on the rocks…all around the head of this kanyon, and down on either side, as far as we could see, were houses of every conceivable form and size…In the centre of this kanyon, and near the head, was a building 16 or 20 feet square; four stories high, and built upon a flat rock about 4 feet higher than the level of the bed of the kanyon…One large building which we entered, stood on the edge of the precipice, with its front wall circular and flush with the bank which formed the back part, making the ground plan of the building like a half moon…"

Huntington gave no precise locations for these cliff dwellings, but from his descriptions it appears that the first ruins they encountered were in Montezuma Canyon, through which flows a northern tributary of the San Juan. The second group must have been one of the imposing groups of ruins preserved at Hovenweep National Monument. Huntington noticed there was no water at the latter site, and he asked his Indian guides "how the former inhabitants could have managed;—they told us they had heard that a very long time ago there was water running here. We asked them who had built these houses. They smilingly shook their heads and said they had never heard…"

All-American Man Pictograph in Salt Creek Canyon, Canyonlands National Park, Utah RANDALL K. ROBERTS

From the time of the arrival of the Spanish in the sixteenth century to about 1880, explorers were very much intrigued by the prehistoric ruins of the Southwest and freely speculated about their origins. Alexander von Humbolt made the startling suggestion that Aztecs left their homeland in Aztlan in 1160 and may have traveled north to the San Juan River country before heading south and settling along the Gila River in Arizona. Some who read Humbolt's book took his hypothesis as fact, and accordingly scattered "Aztecs" and "Montezumas" all over maps of the Southwest. Huntington found his explanation in the *Book of Mormon*. W.H. Bell, whose work carried Powell's account of his 1869 voyage, wrote a chapter on "The Aztec Ruins of New Mexico and Arizona."

Powell and his men were the first explorers to record their observations of ruins in the canyons of the rivers, while W.H. Jackson and W.H. Holmes, working for the Hayden Survey, mapped and described the imposing ruins of both Mesa Verde and Hovenweep. Powell developed a profound and abiding interest in both prehistoric and modern Indians and, as director of the Bureau of American Ethnology, he promoted further archeological research in the Southwest.

Quite naturally, archeologists concentrated first upon the more dramatic and spectacular ruins, and even then much of their work was reconnaissance in character. Little research was done in the canyon country itself until early in the twentieth century. With the passage of the Upper Colorado River Storage Act in 1956, the National Park Service commissioned the University of Utah and the Museum of Northern Arizona to conduct an intensive, seven-year study of prehistoric sites in the Glen and San Juan River canyons that would be inundated by Lake Powell.

Archeologists learned that the American Southwest had been inhabited for at least ten thousand years. From archaic, nomadic, hunter-gatherer beginnings, the Desert culture slowly developed a more complex, cooperative, and sedentary way of life. They learned to cultivate corn, beans, and squash and developed sophisticated irrigation systems to water their crops.

Early settlements consisted of collections of simply constructed, subterranean pit houses. The sophisticated, multi-roomed masonry and wood structures that Huntington and others found were characteristic of the later, Great Pueblo period, which seems to have ended rather abruptly about A.D. 1300. These Ancestral Pueblo sites include the spectacular cliff dwellings of Betatakin, Keet Seel, and Inscription House preserved at Navajo National Monument, Arizona, the splendid structures at Hovenweep National Monument on the Utah/Colorado border, and the extensive ruins at Mesa Verde National Park, Colorado. Scores of other archeological sites dot the canyon country, including dozens that now lie under water in Glen and San Juan River canyons.

The Navajos called the people who preceded them in the canyon country Anasazi, which means —variously—Ancient Ones, Ancient Ancestors, or Enemy Ancestors, depending upon how the term is used in conversation. Archeologists adopted and popularized this term, to the consternation of contemporary Pueblo peoples, who are the most obvious descendants of the Ancient Ones.

Although they are perhaps best known for their architecture, the Ancestral Pueblo people also developed a significant material culture, which included finely woven baskets and beautiful, decorated pottery. Since these early farmers were able to store their crops, they had more leisure time for artistic expression. They painted pictographs and pecked out petroglyphs on the rocks and cliffs that appear to have spiritual significance. They also made jewelry and other objects of adornment from turquoise, imported seashells, and feathers.

For many centuries the Ancestral Pueblo people lived in the upland areas of canyon country, where the conditions of life were better. Only after A.D. 1000 did they begin to move down into the deeper canyons. A swelling population and overcrowding in the more "urban" areas upcountry may have motivated these prehistoric pioneers to head for the canyon country frontier, where they built homes in the recesses of cliff walls and farmed the mesa tops and canyon floors.

Then, something happened. Perhaps it was a prolonged drought; possibly it was the appearance of hostile, nomadic peoples. Whatever the cause, by 1300 the Ancestral Pueblo people abandoned the Colorado Plateau, including sites in the more remote areas of canyon country, and moved south to the Hopi mesas, Zuni, Acoma, and the Rio Grande pueblos.

By the time Domínguez and Escalante ventured into the canyon country in 1776, various other Indian tribes, including the Utes, Paiutes, and Navajos, occupied the land that the Ancestral Pueblo people had deserted. The Utes in particular, with the aid of horses and firearms introduced by the Spanish, held sway over a vast territory extending from the San Juan River country of New Mexico through Colorado to central Utah. Astride the Spanish Trail, the Utes aided and abetted the slave traders and demanded tribute for safe passage. After 1847, when the Mormons fanned out from Salt Lake City, encroaching on Ute territory and putting a stop to the illicit slave trade, the Utes became alarmed. In 1853, they struck back, destroying property and killing several Mormon pioneers throughout central Utah in what has come to be called the Walker War.

Two years later, Utes attacked the isolated, fledgling Elk Mountain Mission and killed three men. The Mormons promptly abandoned their remote canyon country mission. It would be twenty-two years before they would return, this time to stay.

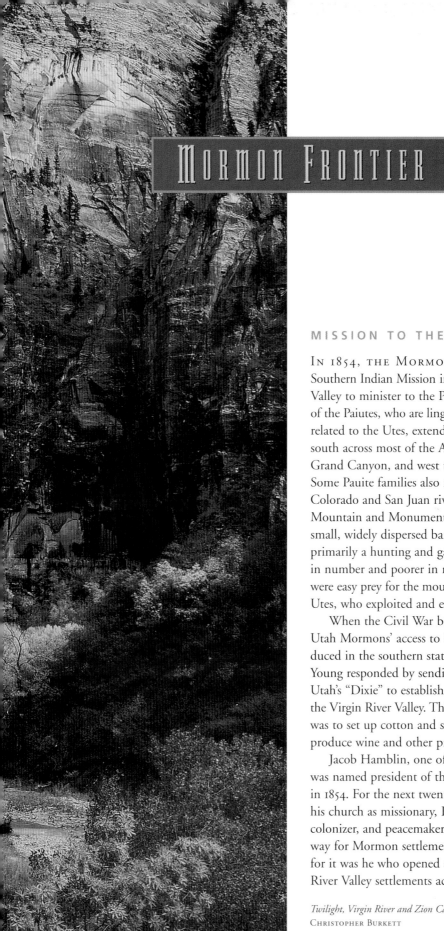

6

MORMON FRONTIER

MISSION TO THE HOPI

IN 1854, THE MORMONS established the Southern Indian Mission in the Santa Clara River Valley to minister to the Paiutes. The homeland of the Paiutes, who are linguistically and culturally related to the Utes, extended from central Utah south across most of the Arizona Strip to the Grand Canyon, and west to the Virgin River. Some Pauite families also resided south of the Colorado and San Juan rivers, between Navajo Mountain and Monument Valley. Living in small, widely dispersed bands, the Paiutes were primarily a hunting and gathering people. Fewer in number and poorer in resources, the Paiutes were easy prey for the mounted and better-armed Utes, who exploited and enslaved them.

When the Civil War broke out in 1861, the Utah Mormons' access to basic commodities produced in the southern states was cut off. Brigham Young responded by sending pioneers south to Utah's "Dixie" to establish a Cotton Mission in the Virgin River Valley. This agricultural enterprise was to set up cotton and sugar plantations and to produce wine and other products.

Jacob Hamblin, one of the first Dixie pioneers, was named president of the nearby Indian Mission in 1854. For the next twenty-nine years, he served his church as missionary, Indian agent, explorer, colonizer, and peacemaker. Hamblin paved the way for Mormon settlement in northern Arizona, for it was he who opened a route from the Virgin River Valley settlements across the Arizona Strip,

Twilight, Virgin River and Zion Canyon, Utah
CHRISTOPHER BURKETT

and from the Colorado River to the Hopi mesas and the upper valley of the Little Colorado.

The groundwork for this Mormon expansion was laid in 1858, when Hamblin was instructed to take a company of men to open relations with the Hopi. Hamblin's party departed Santa Clara in late October and traveled across the open country at the base of the Vermilion Cliffs by way of Pipe Spring to the northern end of the Kaibab Plateau, where they encountered a band of Paiutes. Chief Naraguts and about eighteen men guided Hamblin's party to the Crossing of the Fathers, following practically the same route Domínguez and Escalante had taken eighty-two years earlier.

Hamblin successfully bridged the gap between the Mormon frontier and the Hopi mesas, which constituted the practical limit of Spanish and Mexican influence west of Santa Fe. Reaching the village of Oraibi, the Hamblin party was served "bean soup without a spoon." After visiting the seven Hopi towns, Hamblin left four men behind to preach among the Hopi people and returned to Santa Clara. The four missionaries also returned to the Mormon settlements before spring.

Undeterred by the apparent failure of this first missionary effort, Hamblin led a second mission to Hopi the following year, and a third expedition in 1860.

WAR WITH THE NAVAJOS

Ever since the outbreak of the Mexican War and the arrival of American troops in New Mexico, relations between the Navajos and the newcomers had deteriorated. In 1850, the U.S. Army established a mediating presence at Fort Defiance, in the heart of Navajo country, but Navajo depredations continued. Punitive military operations—launched from Fort Defiance in 1858, 1859, and 1860—ranged north and west and forced the recalcitrant Navajos to retreat and hide out in the canyon country.

It was the Hamblin party's misfortune to be stopped by some of these harried Navajo warriors near Tonalea. Hamblin said later that, in killing young George Albert Smith, the Navajos were avenging the death of some relatives "who had been killed by palefaces like us."

By 1863, an all-out state of war existed. In February of the following year, Colonel Kit Carson and his New Mexico volunteers, implementing a brutally effective scorched earth policy, surrounded the Navajo stronghold of Canyon de Chelly, starved its defenders into submission, and forced them to capitulate. But there were other Navajo warriors who successfully eluded capture and never made the Long Walk to Fort Sumner in eastern New Mexico's Bosque Redondo. These men and their families, led by the Navajo headman Hoskininni, fled to the canyon country and lived among the Paiutes.

Meanwhile, in central Utah, trouble developed between the Mormons and the Utes. The 1865 Black Hawk War cost about seventy lives, destroyed about $1 million in property, and forced the Mormons to abandon many of their frontier settlements. Some of the Navajos who had eluded Kit Carson joined the conflict, along with Paiute bands who had been displaced by Mormon settlement.

In early 1865, the Navajos stole some horses from the new settlement at Kanab, Utah. Paiutes raided the town in December of that same year, and the following February Paiute and Navajo warriors killed J.M. Whitmore and Robert McIntyre near Pipe Spring. A force of the Utah Territorial Militia, headquartered in St. George, chased the latter marauders to the Crossing of the Fathers. There they discovered that the Navajos had made a trail of sand across the frozen river, over which they had led the stolen stock, and made good their escape.

In the spring of 1866, Joseph, Robert, and Isabella Berry were killed by Indians who had raided their homestead in Long Valley, along the East Fork of the Virgin River. Outlying settlements were abandoned.

On August 16, 1866, Captain James Andrus was placed in command of five platoons of cavalry, totaling sixty-two men, and ordered to examine the country north of the Colorado River, from the Kaibab Plateau to the mouth of the Green River. He and his men were to search for any other crossings of the Colorado that Navajo and Paiute raiders might be using and attack any warring parties they encountered. They also were ordered to conciliate with friendly Indians, and to learn

as much as possible about the resources of the country they traversed.

The citizen soldiers were in the saddle for about thirty days. Traveling by way of Pipe Spring and Kanab, one detachment then headed northeast across unknown country before linking up with a second column in the open valley of the Paria River, near the present-day town of Cannonville. Near this rendezvous point, on August 26, Elijah Averett was ambushed and killed while leading two animals across a shallow but precipitous canyon. His comrades buried Elijah there and named the defile Averett Canyon, or Hollow.

While in the Paria River Valley, the militiamen took note of the deeply eroded cliffs of what would later be known as Bryce Canyon. Then they crossed over to the upper valley of the Escalante River and worked their way up to the flat top of the Aquarius Plateau. After riding through groves of pine and aspen, they came out on Bown's Point, also known as Deer Point, where they had an unparalleled view of the canyon country. Adjutant F.B. Woolley described the view:

"Below…to the S.E. is the Colorado Plateau, stretching away as far as the eye can see, a naked barren plain of red and white Sandstone crossed in all directions by innumerable gorges…" He noted occasional high buttes standing above the general level and he could see here and there "the country rising up to the ridges marking the 'breakers' or rocky bluffs of the larger streams. The Sun shining down on this vast red plain almost dazzled our eyes by the reflection as it was thrown back from the fiery furnace."

They could clearly see the Pot-se-Nip Mountains, the earliest known name of this spectacular group that Powell, thinking them unknown, later named the Henry Mountains. From the top of Aquarius, Andrus even thought he could see the mouth of the Green River, but he was mistaken. Having carried out his instructions as nearly as practicable, Andrus and his command returned

Black Mountain aspen forest, Utah Christopher Burkett

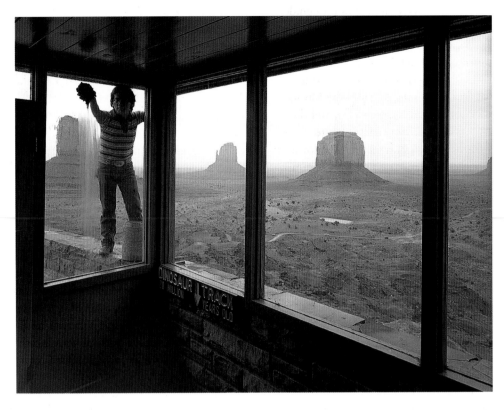

Window washer, Monument Valley Navajo Tribal Park, Arizona-Utah SKEET McAULEY

to St. George by way of the Awapa Plateau, Grass Valley, Circleville, and Parowan.

The war dragged on. Armed patrols, often assisted by friendly Paiutes, guarded the trails between the Colorado and the Mormon frontier. Raiding Navajos and Paiutes typically eluded these guards, and even the detachments of militia sent to punish them.

In the fall of 1869, Jacob Hamblin and a party of forty men, including some Paiute allies, rafted across the Colorado near the mouth of the Paria River, where John D. Lee would later establish his ferry. Their purpose was to visit the Hopi and determine if Indians other than the Navajos were raiding the Mormon settlements. The Hopi told Hamblin that they had learned the Navajos were planning another raid, so he and his men hurried home over the same route. Ironically, had he returned by the more northerly trail, via the Crossing of the Fathers, he would have come face to face with a Navajo raiding party driving as many as fifteen hundred head of stolen stock.

That August, the first Powell expedition had passed through Glen Canyon, but Powell and his men did not encounter any Indians at either the Crossing of the Fathers or the Paria River. When C.H. and Seneca Howland and William Dunn made their fateful decision to leave the Powell expedition at Separation Canyon a month later, they had no idea they would be walking into the middle of a war.

The next summer, Powell recruited Hamblin to escort him to the Shivwits country to learn what had become of the Howlands and Dunn. The resident Paiutes readily admitted that they had executed the intruders. The Paiutes thought Powell's men were murderous miners who had killed a Paiute woman in a drunken brawl on the south side of the Grand Canyon. They didn't believe the men's alibi, that they had just made an unprecedented voyage down the river in boats.

"When white men kill our people, we kill them," the chief explained.

Powell then prevailed on Hamblin to guide him to the Hopi villages, where they enjoyed a lengthy stay. Hamblin, in turn, persuaded Powell to accompany him to Fort Defiance to try to make peace with the Navajos. The two men made a good team. On November 9, 1870, the Mormons and the Indians signed a peace treaty, and the warpath once again became a trade route.

Powell embarked on his second trip down the canyons of the Colorado the following summer, and arrived at the Crossing of the Fathers in early October. While he and his men were camped there, the first Navajo trading party came through en route to the Mormon settlements. Two months later, John D. Lee and his wife Emma—traveling overland from St. George—arrived at the mouth of the Paria River with orders from Hamblin to establish reliable ferry service across the Colorado.

LEE'S FERRY

Lee's Ferry, the dividing point between the upper and lower basins of the Colorado River, is a place of historic and scenic importance. Here, the Colorado dramatically breaks through the Echo Cliffs and leaves the walls of Glen Canyon behind. It sweeps out into the open, with low sandy beaches half a mile long on the south side and two miles long on the north bank. At the mouth of the Paria River, the Colorado tumbles over a huge boulder delta before being swallowed by Marble Canyon.

This was the only place south of Moab where the Colorado was readily accessible, but here the river ran swift and deep and could not be forded. Domínguez and Escalante realized that in 1776, which is why they made their crossing in a less accessible but placid and shallower point upstream. In 1869, Hamblin and his companions became the first to make the crossing here on rafts, but it was

a dangerous undertaking. That same year, the first Powell expedition camped here without giving the place much notice. Hamblin demonstrated the location's potential to Powell the following year, bringing lumber by mule to build a crude boat, which they christened the *Cañon Maid,* by which they crossed the river on the way to Hopi.

In October 1871, Powell ended the first leg of his second expedition here. By the summer of 1872, when Powell arrived to begin the second part of his river trip, Lee was already ferrying occasional travelers across the Colorado.

When Emma Lee first saw her new home, she exclaimed "Oh, what a lonely dell!" And so Lonely Dell it was called for many years thereafter. Lee had been sent to this remote spot after being implicated in the Mountain Meadows Massacre, in which Mormon settlers and Indian allies had wiped out a caravan of California-bound "gentile" pioneers north of St. George. He first built a house, and when spring came he planted some crops and dammed the river to irrigate them.

Until he could build a real ferryboat, Lee first used a crude raft and then the Nellie Powell, a craft Powell had abandoned as being unsuitable for running the river. On January 11, 1873, Lee christened the *Colorado* and inaugurated a regular ferry service. Thus, Lee's Ferry replaced the Crossing of the Fathers as the most practical and direct canyon country crossing of the Colorado between Moab and the mouth of the Virgin River. Lee's Ferry operated here for more than half a century, and during that time ownership passed from Lee to the Church of Jesus Christ of Latter-day Saints, then to the Grand Canyon Cattle Company, and finally to Coconino County, Arizona. In 1929, daily ferry operation ceased when Navajo Bridge was completed across Marble Canyon, six miles downstream.

7

HOLE-IN-THE-ROCK

VILLAGERS UNDER THE RIM

THE EXPANSION of the Mormon frontier, after the arrival of the first pioneers in 1847, was the work of a people determined to extend their spiritual and temporal realm—to build the Kingdom of God in the wilderness. It was a cooperative, planned movement, best described as colonization, in contrast to the haphazard, individualistic character of frontier growth elsewhere in the West.

Brigham Young exhorted the faithful, telling them that the Kingdom would have to be *built.* Under Young's vigorous direction, colonizing new lands, tilling the soil, reclaiming barren places, and redeeming the earth took on religious significance. The remarkable success of Mormon pioneering in Utah and neighboring areas in the West is a tribute to those resourceful men and women of faith, who accepted ecclesiastical direction and submitted to group discipline in order to establish their Zion.

Mormon colonization followed an accepted pattern. The church issued "calls" to those who were expected to perform "missions." Individuals thus appointed formed companies that would seek, for example, to convert the Indians (the Elk Mountain Mission), to found new industries (the Cotton Mission), or to establish new farming communities. Such companies were expected to be self sufficient, and so they were composed of individuals who had demonstrable and diverse skills.

Upon reaching its destination, a company was expected to lay out a community patterned after

Hole-in-the-Rock, Glen Canyon, Utah, ca. 1950s
TAD NICHOLS

Salt Lake City, which itself was modeled after the "Plat of the City of Zion," first used by Mormons in the Midwest. Each new village was laid out on a square, with wide streets, a central public area, and equal-sized lots. Each family's lot was big enough to support a cow or two, chickens, a vegetable garden, and fruit trees.

Although this village plan was developed before the Mormons move to Utah, it was well suited to the needs of the frontier colonies. It facilitated defense, since the first structure to be built in most new villages in the wilderness was a fort. It also afforded an intimate social and cultural life centered on the church, also one of the first buildings to be erected. Such formally organized farm-villages were uncommon elsewhere in the United States, but they became ubiquitous on the Mormon frontier.

Interestingly enough, the Mormon farm-village plan also had an antecedent in the communities of ancestral and contemporary Pueblo peoples of the Southwest.

After Jacob Hamblin and John Wesley Powell made peace with the Navajos at Fort Defiance in 1870, Mormon settlers began moving in earnest into the fertile country at the base of the High Plateaus. In less than a generation, Mormons had established settlements and were farming virtually all of the arable lands on the western edge of the canyon country.

There were three places along the Paria River where farming was possible: One of them was John and Emma Lee's Lonely Dell. Another was a seven-mile-long, half-mile-wide valley along the western slope of the Cockscomb, where the towns of Paria and Adairville were established in 1870 and 1873, respectively. The most successful settlements were Cannonville and Henrieville, established in 1874 in the Paria amphitheater at the base of the plateau.

In 1875, settlers from Sevier Valley crossed over the nine thousand-foot-high saddle between the Table Cliff and Aquarius plateaus to settle Escalante, at the headwaters of the Escalante River, and Boulder, along Boulder Creek. From the Great Basin, settlers crossed the Awapa Plateau to colonize the Fremont River Valley. Traveling downstream, these pioneers founded numerous communities, including Fremont, Loa, Bicknell, Cainville, and Hanksville.

Militiamen pursuing Ute raiders during the 1865 Black Hawk War recognized the potential of Castle Valley, but settlement did not begin in earnest there until 1877. Ferron, Castle Dale, Orangeville, Huntington, and Price were among the earliest towns to be established along the headwaters of the Muddy, San Rafael, and Price rivers, respectively.

HOLE-IN-THE-ROCK

The Mormons' vigorous frontier colonization efforts after 1870 were partly motivated by growing hostility between the Saints and the non-Mormons—the gentiles. The transcontinental railroad, completed in 1869, and the discovery of gold and silver in the interior West, brought many gentiles into the territory. Tensions over matters such as polygamy and politics suggested the desirability of extending the Kingdom as rapidly as possible and ensuring Mormon supremacy in all parts of it.

After the failure of the Elk Mountain Mission in 1855, Mormon settlement was directed southward to the Virgin River and then eastward across the Colorado by way of Lee's Ferry. But by 1877 events east of the Colorado River, in the Four Corners area, compelled the Mormons to re-establish a presence there.

The Hayden Survey publicized the region, and the accompanying maps showed the main trails and roads. Prospectors were rushing into southwestern Colorado, farmers were beginning to settle along the open valley of the San Juan in northwestern New Mexico, and cattlemen from as far away as Texas were tapping the range in southeastern Utah. Moreover, the Utes and Navajos were getting restive.

To establish a foothold in the distant southeastern corner of the territory, the Church of Jesus Christ of Latter-day Saints organized a mission to first select a site, then to found a settlement. The church issued a call in December 1878 at Parowan, and in March 1879 at Cedar City—both older Great Basin towns dating from the 1850s. In April 1879, Silas S. Smith led a vanguard expedition from Paragonah, near Cedar City, to search for a suitable place to settle along the San Juan River.

Smith and his party crossed the Colorado at Lee's Ferry and traveled south along the Echo Cliffs to Moenkopi. At this point, they turned northeast and opened a wagon road through the Navajo country to the San Juan. There, at the confluence with Montezuma Creek, they found a Mormon homesteader, Peter Shurtz, and two gentile families. Leaving some of their number at the San Juan, the explorers returned by a comparatively easy route, which took them north to the Spanish Trail. They crossed the Colorado near the site of the abandoned Elk Mountain Mission, where they also found a few hearty homesteaders, then followed the Spanish Trail back to Paragonah.

The Smith party traveled nearly a thousand miles in a great circle and it had established a trail that would be passable for wagons. But, faced with the prospect of making the same roundabout trip to Montezuma Creek, the main colonizing expedition chose to attempt a shortcut. As final preparations were being made at Parowan, Reuben Collett and Andrew P. Schow reported that it was possible to take a more direct route by way of their Mormon frontier town of Escalante, established just four years earlier.

It was no small task to take eighty-three fully loaded wagons over the Escalante Rim of the Straight Cliffs and thence forty miles southeast across the open desert at the base of Fifty Mile Mountain to Forty Mile Spring. But finally, in November 1879, more than two hundred fifty men, women, and children and a thousand head of livestock were assembled and ready to jump off.

During the wait at Forty Mile Spring, the pioneers held several dances on a huge sandstone stage they dubbed Dance Hall Rock. But soon, ominous news dampened the festive mood. They learned that, contrary to assurances of Collett and Schow, the country ahead had not been thoroughly explored. The great gorge of Glen Canyon loomed about twenty-five miles ahead and, even if they could find a place to cross, no one knew what they would encounter on the other side of Colorado River.

But early snows on the High Plateaus blocked their return, so there was no turning back.

Arriving at the Colorado, two and a half miles south of the mouth of the Escalante River, pathfinders found a natural fault on the rim of Glen Canyon. It was just a narrow slit at its head, but it opened out into a very short, steep tributary canyon. By blasting, the Mormons enlarged the crack wide enough for the wagons to get through. The spot is still known as Hole-in-the-Rock, and the trail from Escalante is likewise known today as Hole-in-the-Rock Road.

The descent over the west rim of Glen Canyon was the most serious obstacle the pioneers encountered on the entire trek. After widening the Hole-in-the-Rock, they had to cut back into the fifty-five-foot, solid sandstone cliff face to build a road grade feasible for wagons. Below the base of the hole, there was nothing but a narrow declivity at the head of the canyon and steep slopes on bare rock on either side. The Mormons constructed a narrow road along the left slope by blasting and digging, and shored up the grade on the canyon side. At one seemingly impassable spot, where there was nothing more than a narrow ledge on a near-perpendicular wall, the men built a cantilever road by setting oak logs into the cliff face and "paving" the road with wooden stringers. Beyond the halfway point, the pioneers were able to slide the wagons down a steep but sandy slope.

The vertical drop from Hole-in-the-Rock to the water's edge was one thousand feet. It took Smith's party six weeks to build the rim-to-river road, which was about as long as they had expected their entire journey to Montezuma Creek to take. Beginning on January 28, 1880, the entire caravan of eighty-three wagons drove through the hole and down the makeshift cliff-face road. As the indefatigable historian, Andrew Jenson, wrote after visiting Hole-in-the-Rock in 1928, "How they ever got their wagons down that steep incline will puzzle all future generations."

Once in Glen Canyon, it was necessary to get out on the other side. Charles Hall assembled a ferryboat and the entire expedition, two wagons at a time, was rowed across the Colorado. The way out was difficult enough, but they were able to make it in stages. First they built a dugway from the river up to a two hundred fifty-foot-high bench. Then they chopped out a road up a short

Thunderstorm, Indian Creek Valley, Utah LARRY ANGIER

side canyon to the head of Cottonwood Creek. Next they constructed another dugway and widened "Little-Hole-in-the-Rock" to climb Cottonwood Hill. From Cheese Camp, they climbed up the narrow Chute to the base of Grey Mesa, and then excavated several short dugways to reach the top of the mesa. There, they found snow two feet deep.

The view from the top of Grey Mesa that cold February day was breathtaking, but the travelers scarcely had time to admire it. They traveled along the southern rim of the mesa, overlooking the Big Bend of the San Juan River in a canyon a thousand feet deep. Behind them, the Straight Cliffs of the Kaiparowits Plateau reminded them of the weeks of toil that had brought them this far. To the south, across the San Juan, Navajo Mountain stood out boldly on the skyline. Ahead of them was an endless confusion of rock and sand, mesas and slick rock. There were few trees.

"It's nothing in the world but rocks and holes, hills and hollows. The mountains are just one

solid rock …" wrote Elizabeth Decker to relatives back home.

On February 21, in the midst of a bad blizzard on Grey Mesa, Olivia Larson gave birth to a baby boy while lying on the spring seat of a wagon. Baby John Rio Larson, born within site of his namesake San Juan, was the third child born since the trek began. Three days later, the Larsons caught up with the rest of the wagon train.

A startled mountain sheep inadvertently showed guides a way off Grey Mesa, The route down was steep but passable and led to a pleasant surprise: half-mile-long Lake Pagahrit, formed by a natural dam on the upper course of Lake Canyon. The travelers stopped to rest and catch up on their laundry, and then crossed over the dam and went on.

After leaving the lake, it was a rather easy pull up Castle Creek Wash, which they named for a prehistoric ruin they passed along the way, to Clay Hill Pass. From there, they could look far ahead across the Grand Gulch Plateau, but the goal was not in sight. After building a steep road down Clay Hill, they took a sight on Bear's Ears to the northeast and circled the north end of Grand Gulch, east of what is now Natural Bridges National Monument.

Dense forests of juniper, pinyon, and cedar carpeted the landscape at this point. Scouting the route was exceedingly difficult, and the pathfinders had to cut down trees to let the wagons by. As the pioneers headed south down the Comb Wash, they could see the Abajo Mountains on the eastern horizon. This was encouraging because they had been told this landmark range was within sight of their destination.

They reached the bed of Comb Wash only to find the one thousand-foot-high cliff of Comb Ridge barring their path. Turning south, they traveled for nearly twenty miles down the sandy wash without finding a pass through the ridge. Finally, they arrived at the San Juan, only to discover that the river had cut a canyon through the ridge and the walls were too steep to reach the stream.

They couldn't go down, so they had to go up and over Comb Ridge. It took three days to build dugways up what the pioneers named "San Juan Hill." Seven teams to the wagon pulled and clawed up the steep, slick-rock road, slipping and falling to their knees. But, goaded and whipped, they finally topped the grade. After building more dugway to get across Butler Wash, the weary travelers

reached the open, sandy banks of the San Juan. They soon came to Cottonwood Wash, crossed it, and camped on the flat bottomlands.

It was April 6, 1880, only eighteen miles to go, and open road all the way. But they had had all they could take. They had spent four months— the entire winter—on what was supposed to have been a six-week journey, and they had blazed a trail the entire way. Everyone, including the three babies born en route, had survived the trip, but all were exhausted.

"We'll stay here," they agreed. After all, there was plenty of water, wood, and arable land. So, that evening they selected a spot to establish a village, which they would call Bluff City. Platte D. Lyman wrote in his diary: "Wednesday, April 7th, 1880. We began laying off the lots and land and most of the brethren began work on the ditch."

For about a year after the Hole-in-the-Rock colonizing expedition crossed Glen Canyon, the road they built served as a main link between the new settlements at Bluff and Montezuma Canyon and the older communities from whence the trekkers had come. The road supported two-way traffic, although this fact seems incredible when one looks at surviving sections of the road today. Many of these, such as San Juan Hill, are particularly difficult to reach. At best, the road between Escalante and Bluff crossed some of the most rugged parts of the canyon country and was one of the longest, roughest wagon roads in the West.

8

THE ROCK JUNGLE

TWISTING THE MULE

THROUGH 1880, CHARLES HALL continued
to operate a ferry at Hole-in-the-Rock Crossing
while also scouting an alternative route to and
across the Colorado River. He finally found one
thirty-five miles upstream at a place known ever
since as Hall's Crossing, just above the mouth
of Hall's Creek and east of the Waterpocket Fold.
At this point, the walls of Glen Canyon were low
and the river was much easier to approach from
either side.

Charles Hall most likely worked out the wagon
road from Escalante to the new crossing. Travelers
embarking from Escalante would be given the
following directions:

Stay on Hole-in-the-Rock Road for ten miles
and then turn east and follow Harris Wash as it
drops into a canyon. At its mouth you will find
yourself at the Escalante River. Go upstream nearly
half a mile to the mouth of a narrow canyon,
which is Silver Falls Creek. Ford the Escalante
there and head up the slick rock canyon and into
a pinyon and juniper forest. The trees obscure
the view, and you can easily get lost, but keep on
climbing. Soon you will top out and can get your
bearings. You have just come through the rough
country enclosed by the Circle Cliffs. Off to the
north is the dark rim of Boulder Mountain, and
those isolated gray-green peaks to the east are the
Henry Mountains.

The roughest part of the road is just ahead.
Below you is a huge, funnel-like opening between

Halls Creek Valley and Waterpocket Fold,
Capitol Reef National Park, Utah LARRY ULRICH

two cliffs. Drive down over that steep slope and head for the funnel. Over the next two miles you will descend one thousand feet. You are in a deep, narrow canyon now, with one sharp bend after another, and the cliff walls are undercut at nearly every turn. You might have to do some roadwork to get your wagons through this Muley Twist Canyon, but it will get you through the otherwise impenetrable Waterpocket Fold.

Keep going. That open sky ahead is the valley of Hall's Creek. When you exit Muley Twist Canyon, turn right and follow Hall's Creek about thirty miles to the Colorado. After you cross at Hall's Ferry, the road isn't bad—about twenty miles over knobby slick rock and hummocks of sand and you'll reach the original Hole-in-the-Rock Road. Then it's about seventy-five miles to Bluff by way of Clay Hills Pass, Grand Flat, Comb Wash, and San Juan Hill.

From Escalante, Charles Hall brought in logs, planks, and pitch to make a crude, tapered, thirty-foot-long boat. There was neither a cable nor a rope to guide the craft. It was towed upstream and then shoved off with the payload. One man steered while two others paddled as the boat angled down-stream toward the opposite bank. Hall charged about five dollars per wagon and seventy-five cents each for horses. He lived on Escalante Road, eight miles from the crossing at the base of the Waterpocket Fold. When customers came down the trail, he would walk down to the crossing and ferry them across. Travelers arriving from the south side of the river sometimes had to wait for service.

There were never enough travelers to sustain Hall's ferry business, and he finally decided to abandon it in 1884. On March 30, 1883, the last spike completing the Denver & Rio Grande Western Railroad was driven a few miles west of Green River, Utah, fittingly on the old Spanish Trail. The completion of this line, connecting Denver with Salt Lake, was particularly significant for the isolated settlements south and east of the Colorado River in Utah. By then,

a good wagon road linked Bluff, Montezuma Creek, and other fledgling communities with the railhead in Durango, Colorado, and it was no longer necessary to travel the pioneer roads across the canyons.

THE ROCK JUNGLE

The coming of the railroads also contributed to a canyon country cattle boom. With an early start in the intermountain West, the Mormon cattle industry prospered meeting the growing demand for meat in the mining camps of California,

Burr Trail through Waterpocket Fold,
Capitol Reef National Park, Utah
STU LEVY

away as Texas were already ranging cattle on the grassy slopes of the Abajo and La Sal mountains. Construction of the railroads stimulated the market, and the opportunity to make unfettered use of the public domain for grazing enabled the cattle barons to make tremendous profits—as much as 50 percent in the 1870s and 1880s—with a minimal investment. The economics were simple: Buy a herd of longhorns at rock bottom prices in Texas, trail them to the nearest unappropriated open range, squat on it, let the herd multiply, sell the increase, and buy more stock.

In the late 1870s, outfits headed by Pat O'Donel, Spud Hudson, the Widow Lacey, and Harold and Edmund Carlisle came to southeastern Utah to capitalize on the beef bonanza. The Carlisles managed the Utah operations of the Kansas and New Mexico Land and Cattle Company, a huge, English-owned and London-headquartered concern operating in Kansas, Colorado, New Mexico, and Utah.

Not to be outdone, Mormon cattlemen traveled over the Spanish Trail and arrived at the vicinity of the Elk Mountain Mission in 1877. They found the mission fort occupied by two trapper/prospectors: William Granstaff, who called himself "Nigger Charlie," and a Canadian known simply as Frenchie. After a brief stay, the cattlemen moved further south to the base of the La Sal Mountains, where they built a settlement in 1878. Others, bringing up the rear the following year, established the town of Moab near the Elk Mountain Mission.

The pioneers at Bluff also entered the business, working their cattle cooperatively in the "Bluff Pool." The colony struggled as an agricultural community because the San Juan River periodically would cut away its own terraces and take the fertile farmlands with it. However, it prospered as a cow town. In the late 1880s, some residents moved

Nevada, Colorado, and elsewhere. In the 1870s, as Mormon pioneers moved south and east from the Great Basin to the periphery of the canyon country, cattle and sheep were put on the open ranges.

The Mormons took a particular interest in raising sheep because their wool was a renewable resource, and they also could be used for food. The green acres around each village were usually irrigated and planted with forage crops to provide winter feed for range stock and dairy herds.

When the Mormons arrived in Bluff in 1880, they found that enterprising cattlemen from as far

upcountry to Verdure and Monticello to be closer to the best ranges, and when irrigation canals diverting water from the Abajo Mountains were completed in 1905, the town of Blanding was founded.

As the cattle industry expanded, cowboys began to range herds further west, into the rugged lands sloping off toward the Colorado River, including Indian Creek, Beef Basin, Dark Canyon, White Canyon, Red Canyon, and the wedge-shaped country west of the Clay Hills and north of the San Juan River.

Cattle were wintered at these lower elevations and were driven down into the lower canyons and bottomlands wherever accessible. The country below the pinyon and juniper forests was warmer, but it provided very poor forage for the herds. There was too much rock and not enough grass, so it would take more than two hundred acres to support just one cow, or five sheep. Often, animals would get lost in the canyons, become rimrocked, and die of thirst within site of water.

Dead Horse Point commemorates not one but a whole herd of horses that perished there.

"A rock jungle" is how J.A. Scorup characterized The Needles, Dark Canyon, the Woodenshoe, and the Clay Hills, where his outfit ranged its stock.

The territory southeast of the Colorado River was a wild place where the frontiers from east and west collided. There was open range warfare between the little guy and the big outfit, plus Indian troubles and rustling. The canyon country was actually ideal for rustlers, who could rope cows and run a brand with little chance of being seen. Indeed, in the early days, all a man really needed to get started in the cattle business was a good horse and a long rope.

Rustling became especially popular after the Denver & Rio Grande Western Railroad was completed in 1883, and so did train robbery. Robber's Roost was a favorite hideout for assorted rustlers and train and bank robbers, most notably Butch Cassidy and the Wild Bunch. Robber's Roost was remote and practically inaccessible on

jewelry and distinctive woolen blankets and rugs. With the completion of the Atchison, Topeka and Santa Fe Railway in the 1880s, the market for high-quality, Navajo-made goods mushroomed.

The population increasing and their industries growing, The People were soon moving into areas beyond the formal bounds of their reservation. In the ten-year period after 1878, they moved in ever-increasing numbers into lands along the San Juan River. The Navajos appear to have gotten along well with the Paiutes who already lived there, and were able to cross through their neighbors' territory to reach the north side of the San Juan and Colorado rivers. Stories are told that Navajos routinely crossed the rivers to hunt in the Henry Mountains, and the Clay Hill Crossing-White Canyon trail would have been the most direct route.

Once the Mormons completed the road across Glen Canyon at Hole-in-the-Rock, Navajos and Paiutes began to use it to travel to the Mormon settlements to trade, and to hunt on the Kaiparowits Plateau. When the Mormons arrived on the San Juan, the Navajos were already running sheep on Elk Ridge. Not long after the founding of Bluff, Kumen Jones went up on the ridge seeking a summer cattle range. Not far from the Bear's Ears he found Navajo headman Kigalia camped at the spring that still bears his name.

two sides, and there was a spring and plenty of grass. It was also reasonably close to Hanksville, whose merchants were more than happy to do business with the gangs.

THE CANYONS OF THE PEOPLE

In 1868, the Navajos who were interred at Fort Sumner, New Mexico, concluded a treaty with the U.S. government and were permitted to return to a newly established reservation that incorporated much of their traditional territory. They rejoined their brethren Diné—The People—who had successfully avoided capture by fleeing to the west. In 1870, these western Navajo bands also concluded a separate treaty, negotiated by Jacob Hamblin and Maj. John Wesley Powell, in which they promised to cease raiding the Mormon settlements in Utah.

With peace came greater prosperity. The People devoted their energies to raising sheep, goats, and horses. They also made highly desirable trade goods, including fine silver and turquoise

EL DORADO

SIERRA AZUL

THE SANDSTONE COUNTRY of the Colorado
River canyons had long been a lodestone. In the
late seventeenth century, after Diego de Vargas
re-established Spanish rule in New Mexico, he
exchanged letters with the Viceroy about the Sierra
Azul, or Blue Mountain. Vargas believed there
must be a rich mine of quicksilver somewhere in
the province of the Hopi, and over time others
speculated about gold and silver, as well.

The Sierra Azul eluded those who sought it,
although Father Escalante reportedly was shown
a sample of quicksilver ore before he and Father
Domínguez began their expedition to Utah. They
undoubtedly kept the fabled Blue Mountain in
mind while traveling through the land of the
Yutas (Utes). But it wasn't until they reached Glen
Canyon and the Crossing of the Fathers that they
spotted it on the southern horizon: the blue dome
of Navajo Mountain, El Cerro Azul as Miera y
Pacheco would so name it on his map.

For ten years after gold was discovered in
California in 1848, Americans rushed headlong
across the continent in hopes of striking it rich.
Then, when gold was found in Colorado, at the
eastern base of the Rocky Mountains, in 1858, and
near Pike's Peak the following year, prospectors
realized that the precious metal might be found
anywhere in the West.

About a year after the Pike's Peak Rush, Charles
Baker arrived in the San Juan Mountains of southwestern Colorado to prospect. After taking time

Needles Overlook, Canyonlands National Park, Utah
GEORGE H.H. HUEY

out to serve in the Civil War, Baker and two companions returned to the San Juan country in 1867. They had worked their way some distance down the San Juan River when Indians attacked them. The sole survivor was James White, who claims to have rafted the San Juan and Colorado rivers in 1867 to make good his escape. The reports of White's rescue carried the news that Baker's party had been prospecting, and this undoubtedly had something to do with the rush to the San Juan Mountains.

During the summer of 1872, the nation was titillated by reports that diamonds, rubies, and sapphires had been found somewhere in the West. Most of these early reports, though vague, seemed to locate the diamonds in northeastern Arizona, in the vicinity of Fort Defiance, or near the Hopi villages, or along the San Juan River near the mouth of Chinle Creek, or in Monument Valley, or near Navajo Mountain. The few published

reports of Powell's 1869 voyage were searched for clues. Ex-governor William Gilpin of Colorado delivered an address and announced that the diamond fields were in southwestern Colorado. Even South African diamond miners caught the "Arizona Fever." Before the year 1872 ended, Clarence King and his associates on the U.S. Geological Exploration of the Fortieth Parallel found the alleged diamond fields, in northwestern Colorado, and proved them conclusively to be one of the most ingenious hoaxes ever pulled off in the West.

And yet the story proved too good to die. So what if one of the claims had been salted? What about all those other reports of diamonds and other precious stones that had been found elsewhere? Didn't someone say diamonds had been found in proximity to those ruined cities that some people thought the Aztecs had built? The original treasure trove of Montezuma! Many prospectors

John F. Steward, member of the 1871-72 Powell Survey team, in Glen Canyon
JOHN K. HILLERS

Peering over Comb Ridge, Near Bluff, Utah MARK KLETT

carried on the search, adding diamonds to their dreams of gold and silver. For years, these legendary diamond fields remained on the maps of northeastern Arizona.

PISH-LA-KI

New Year's Eve, 1879. James Merrick and Ernest Mitchell met a party of five Mormon scouts north of the San Juan River on the eastern slope of Comb Ridge. The scouts were trailblazers for the wagon train that was making its way from Hole-in-the-Rock, and were on their way back from Montezuma Creek to join the main party. One of these scouts, George Hobbs, struck up a conversation with Merrick and learned that the two men were prospectors who knew that the Navajos had a smelter that was handling ore that assayed at 90 percent silver. They were on their way to search

for the mine. Mitchell, Merrick, and the Mormons crossed the Comb Ridge and parted company at the mouth of Comb Wash. The prospectors then forded the San Juan, headed south toward Monument Valley, and disappeared.

For more than a decade, ever since the Navajos imprisoned at Fort Sumner were permitted to return to their homeland, tales about hidden silver mines had drifted off the reservation. The Navajos had become adept at making silver belt buckles, buttons, clasps, and jewelry, which led prospectors to ask: "Where was the source for the silver?" Merrick, for one, thought he knew where to find it.

Time passed, but the two men did not return. An armed search party sent to look for Mitchell and Merrick found their bodies, covered with rocks and brush, near the spectacular Monument Valley buttes that now bear their names. Local Navajos said the Paiutes had killed the white men,

Paiutes in the vicinity pleaded innocent and blamed the Navajos. Specimens of very rich quartz ore were found near their bodies, which strongly suggested that the men had indeed discovered a mine and had been killed before they could return with the news.

The legendary silver mine of the Navajos became identified with the presumed discovery by Merrick and Mitchell, and one prospecting party after another from southwestern Colorado tried to locate the mine where the two men were supposed to have found the silver ore. Colorado newspapers played up the story. On April 14, 1882, the *Rocky Mountain News* reported that, in one of the canyons leading into the Colorado, they had "found old Indian smelters, but saw nothing of the fabled Myrick (Merrick-Mitchell) mine…

They also discovered a large ledge of silver-bearing ore, ten feet in thickness and one hundred feet in width in proximity to the smelters…Mortars in which the ore was ground were discovered in the rocks close at hand, also sledge hammers of stone with wooden handles…The fabulous richness of the Navajo mountains is true beyond a peradventure."

In 1882 the *Rocky Mountain News* reported that a party of seven had left Durango, Colorado, to take possession of a "great copper mine which was discovered by Cass Hite on his exploring tour a few weeks ago. This is known to be a lode of mammoth size…A competent assayer finds 49 percent of metallic copper in the specimens, and about $17 besides in silver and gold. This from the surface. How much richer it will prove from

Goosenecks of the San Juan River, Utah   Jay Dusard

working further in and down, each mining expert will guess for himself." When it came to a name for the discovery, Hite said the vein "in commemoration of his predecessors…should be called the Merrick and Mitchell lode."

Hite and his party, which included George M. Miller, James E. Porter, and Joseph Duckett, may have found some of the copper deposits. They existed in sedimentary sandstone at the northern foot of Hoskininni Mesa at the head of Copper Canyon, through which flows a southern tributary of the San Juan. While Hite worked the "Merrick and Mitchell lode," others of the party ranged out through the canyons and over the mesas to Navajo Mountain. At one place at the eastern foot of Navajo Mountain, G.M. Miller carved his name and the date, 1882, on a rock.

Hite became acquainted with Navajo chief Hoskininni, headman in the Copper Canyon region. Evidently, Hite's copper mine hadn't panned out well, because he queried Hoskininni about the possible location of a silver mine elsewhere that might prove to be the Mitchell-Merrick mine. He was so persistent that the Navajos began to call him "Hosteen Pish-la-ki," which means Mr. Silver Hunter or Mr. Silver. Hoskininni told Hite that the Navajos had a secret silver mine but that he would not tell him the location of it. If Hite was so anxious to find metal, the chief asked, why didn't he go to the great canyon of the Colorado? There he would find gold in the sands of the river. Hoskininni would show him the way. The chief was right. With Cass Hite, he traveled by way

of White Canyon to the Colorado and there they found some gold in the banks of the river.

Men kept looking for the Mitchell-Merrick mine long after Hite gave up the search. It even came to be known as the Pish-la-ki mine. All the elements of a good lost mine story were present: the hazy Spanish myth of Sierra Azul, the supposed discovery of the mine and the killing of Merrick and Mitchell, and the wild country where the Indians guarded the secret of their mine. Bring together those who have been in the country for some time, who know the mesas west of Monument Valley and the intricate slopes of Navajo Mountain, and they will suggest where they think the mine is, or was, located.

Well into the twentieth century, the Navajos were still keeping a wary eye out for treasure hunters. In 1911, chief Hoskininni and about fifty other Navajo men stopped a party surveying the Arizona-Utah boundary to ask them if they were searching for the "money rock," the silver of "Pash Leki," surveyor Francis John Dyer reported.

GOLD IN GLEN CANYON

In 1883, the quest suddenly shifted from silver to gold when Cass Hite discovered the latter mineral in Glen Canyon. According to the *Rocky Mountain News,* Hite was "a mining prospector of sixteen years experience, of superior education, of equal industry and capacity for hardship and toil…" He was thirty-eight when he first went to Glen Canyon and he lived there for the next thirty-one years, longer than any other person.

Hite entered Glen Canyon by way of White Canyon and crossed the Colorado at the spot that today bears his name. He called it "Dandy's Crossing." There were a number of prehistoric sites in the vicinity, including a multi-storied building that overlooked the mouth of White Canyon. In Hite's day, it became known as "Fort Moqui" and was the most popular tourist attraction in Glen Canyon before it was sub-merged by Lake Powell. The number of ancient sites in the area suggests that the crossing was well known to prehistoric peoples, as it was to the Navajos who directed Hite here.

Shortly after arriving at the Colorado, Hite discovered placer gold in the gravel banks on both sides of the river. More extensive explorations up and down the river soon turned up more gold. There probably had been some inconsequential prospecting in the canyons below Moab and Green River and above Lee's Ferry between the time Powell made his second voyage and Hite's arrival. But it was Hite's discovery that created excitement and led to a mild Glen Canyon gold rush.

The first phase of this Glen Canyon gold rush lasted about seven years, during which time several hundred men prospected this rugged region. The area was so far beyond the reach of the long arm of territorial law enforcement that the miners established and enforced their own.

On December 3, 1883, nine men, including Hite as secretary, signed their names to bylaws governing the Henry Mountains Mining District. The district boundaries followed the Colorado River from the mouth of the Dirty Devil to Hall's Crossing, north from there along the Waterpocket Fold to the "Big Sandy" or Fremont River, and thence to its confluence with the Colorado. The regulations specified the amount of "discovery work" necessary to establish and hold a claim, qualifications for membership, and penalties for claim jumping and "other fraudulent or dishonor-able conduct." In 1887, the White Canyon Mining District was organized along similar lines, with Hite again serving as secretary. This district adjoined the Henry Mountains Mining District at the Colorado and included an area of comparable size southeast of the river.

During the 1880s, prospectors in Glen Canyon found gold all along the Colorado, from the mouth of the Dirty Devil to Lee's Ferry. But it was extremely fine and difficult to recover by ordinary methods of panning and sluicing. The gold dust tended to float on the surface of the water and was easily lost during the washing process. The best locations were on the gravel terraces above the high-water level. Prior to 1890, the more productive placers were found at Dandy Crossing Bar, Ticaboo Bar, Good Hope Bar, and California Bar.

The presence of placer gold in Glen Canyon naturally caused miners to speculate about its source, and soon prospectors began to work their

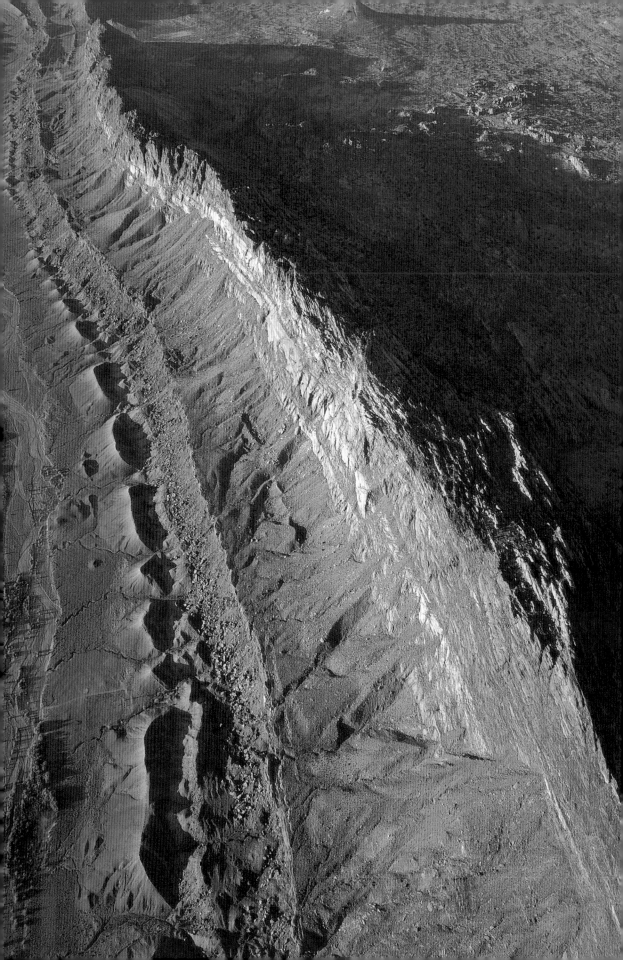

way up the canyons to the laccolithic mountains. Even though the land in Utah south of the San Juan River was added to the Navajo Reservation in 1884, occasional prospecting parties climbed up Navajo Mountain to look for the lost mine of Pish-la-ki. Others hopefully examined the Henry Mountains for gold, despite the fact that Grove K. Gilbert had already issued a pessimistic appraisal in his geological report, which was incorporated into Maj. John Wesley Powell's survey. Gilbert theorized that gold in paying quantities would not be found there.

But who cared about theory when one could find color in the washes. Not Jack Sumner. Jack had been with Powell on the 1869 trip and had kept his eyes open for minerals. In fact, Sumner probably panned for gold here and there along the way but, like most prospectors, he would not have expected to find good diggings in sandstone country. Nonetheless, he came back to Glen Canyon and, in 1889, he and Jack Butler discovered gold in the Bromide Basin on Mt. Ellen. There was a rush to the Henry Mountains, the boomtown of Eagle City sprang up, some gold was found, but the mines soon played out. Gilbert had been right.

To the prospector, the geology of the entire canyon region was confusing. It was chiefly sandstone, yet Hite had found copper in sedimentary rocks in Copper Canyon, and gold in the sand and gravel of Glen Canyon. What kind of country was this? Powell and his corps of brilliant assistants —Dutton, Gilbert, Howell, and Thompson— already had found out. Their classic monographs on the geologic history of the Colorado Plateau stated many of its fundamental facts, followed by sound interpretation and generalizations, which have been elaborated upon by later students.

The Colorado Plateau has been shaped principally by water-based erosion of gigantic masses of sedimentary rock. This is not a static condition—vigorous erosion continues today. During the Paleozoic and Mesozoic eras, a span of a mere four hundred ninety million years, the plateau of today was a flat area near the sea on

which sediments were deposited. As the beds were laid down, they apparently sank under water entirely. At the close of the Cretaceous era (the last period of the Mesosoic) about sixty million years ago, the plateau area was pushed upward in a huge block. This block remained fairly level, although there was some warping and folding of the sandstone beds. Following the uplift, a long cycle of erosion reduced the block to a nearly flat, sea level plain.

In the Tertiary period of the Cenozoic era, thicker beds of sediment were deposited over the area, and a drainage system developed across these beds that was the precursor to the Colorado River. There was a subsequent period of uplift, during which the huge block of bedded sandstone was raised to about its present height above sea level and some faulting occurred. Because of the uplift, the gradients of streams were increased and the rivers began to cut vigorously down through the upraised block. The intricate, dissected canyon country landscape we see today is the result of about twenty million years of stream erosion. This wearing away has been so profound that the folds and warping which occurred during the Cretaceous period have come to the surface and can be seen clearly in the San Rafael Swell, the Waterpocket Fold, the Echo Cliffs, Comb Ridge, and in some of the other prominent features of the landscape. During the last erosion cycle, huge masses of molten rock pushed up through the sedimentary strata and bulged them but did not break through the layers. The molten rock cooled and solidified. As erosion proceeded, it left these as laccolithic mountains, standing high above the sandstone plateaus.

The gold that Sumner and Butler found in the Bromide Basin came from the hard, exposed magma near the top of Mt. Ellen. But it is unlikely that the Henry Mountains were the source of the gold dust found in Glen Canyon. Geologists seem to think these traces of gold were deposited in the sedimentary beds during the early periods of the Mesozoic era and were washed free as later erosion occurred.

10

Canyon Conquest

HO! FOR THE SAN JUAN

CASS HITE DID WHAT HE COULD to stimulate interest in mining Glen Canyon, writing letters to the *Salt Lake Tribune* and other newspapers and soliciting investment capital. His efforts also may have led, indirectly, to the formation of the Denver, Colorado Canyon, and Pacific Railroad Company, which was established on March 25, 1889 in Denver.

As its name suggests, the corporation envisioned building a water-level railroad through the canyons of the Colorado River from Grand Junction, Colorado, to the western seaboard to connect the coalfields of the Rocky Mountains with Southern California. President Frank B. Brown took charge of the initial survey expedition, and Robert Brewster Stanton—a prominent railroad engineer—signed on to determine the feasibility of the idea and assess the resources along the route.

In May 1889, Brown, Stanton, and sixteen companions left Green River, Utah, in six boats. After losing some of their boats in the rapids of Cataract Canyon, they managed to reach Hite Crossing in June. From there, the survey team floated another fourteen miles downstream to Ticaboo Creek, where they found Cass Hite mining the sandy bank. The expedition rested and repaired their badly battered boats, while Brown and Stanton noted everything of possible interest to the railroad.

The party surveyed about half of Glen Canyon and concluded their intensive study at a place now

Robert Brewster Stanton (right) and party conducting railroad survey in Glen Canyon, Utah FRANKLIN A. NIMS

Hite Crossing, Glen Canyon, Utah, ca. 1950s TAD NICHOLS

known as Mystery Canyon, where some of the men inscribed their names. After pausing briefly at Lee's Ferry in early July, the expedition entered treacherous Marble Canyon, where disaster struck. Brown and two others were drowned when their boat capsized.

Undaunted by this tragedy, Stanton returned before the year was out to continue the survey. He brought new boats overland and launched them at Hite Crossing. Stanton met with Hite again and noted the intrepid miner's various gold placers along the way. He also encountered Jack Sumner and had a long talk with him about his observations as a member of the 1869 Powell expedition. Stanton resumed the railroad survey in the lower part of Glen Canyon, successfully negotiated Marble and Grand canyons, and made it all the way to the Gulf of California, where the expedition completed its survey in April 1890.

The whole breathtaking concept, and Stanton's achievement in successfully surveying the canyons of the Colorado, attracted much national attention. Although the idea may seem incomprehensible today, Stanton was convinced that constructing a railroad through the canyons was technically feasible and economically practicable, and he argued his case in a lengthy paper he presented before the American Society of Civil Engineers. However, the company was not able to raise the necessary capital, and the scheme was dropped.

Stanton's canyon railroad survey came at a time when considerable development was occurring in Glen Canyon. Cass Hite's brothers John and Ben and Ben's son Homer joined him in the canyon. In 1892, gold and other minerals were discovered in the La Sal, Abajo, and Carrizo mountains, and mines in the Bromide Basin and the Henry Mountains were likewise booming. By year-end, news was trickling out that rich placers had been found on the San Juan River deep in the canyon somewhere downstream from Bluff.

The San Juan was remote and its canyons had not been tested, so people speculated that the San Juan lode might be the elusive Pish-la-ki mine. There were reports of "secret" discoveries and attempt to stake out the whole canyon before the general public caught the gold fever. In November 1892, Navajo Reservation lands west of the 110th meridian were briefly returned to the public domain. By Christmas, newspapers were full of news from the San Juan, and by New Year's Day the rush was on.

All along the Santa Fe Railway in New Mexico and Arizona, towns were nearly depopulated. In southwestern Colorado, Durango residents went wild. Denver & Rio Grande Western executives contemplated extending the line to Bluff, which was enjoying its first boom as the last supply point on the road from Colorado. Other towns along the Denver & Rio Grande Western vied with one another to be the preferred point of departure for miners headed for the San Juan.

Green River, Utah, offered definite advantages. It had served as the jumping-off place for the diggings in Glen Canyon. A road had been opened across the San Rafael Desert to Hanksville, and from there down North Wash to the Colorado above Hite. Now Green River boosters hoped to capitalize on the rush to the San Juan by playing up this established route across Glen Canyon.

But by the end of January, it appeared that the San Juan Rush was a bust. Those who actually reached the river discovered that the reports, like so many before, had been exaggerated and that any good claims already had been staked. The *Salt Lake Tribune* reported that one disillusioned individual had inscribed his feelings on a sandstone block at Navajo Spring, near the base of Comb Ridge: "One hundred dollars reward for the damned fool who started the gold boom."

BOOM TIMES IN THE CANYONS

After the bubble burst, those miners who had staked early claims along the San Juan continued to mine the canyon, but most of the gold mining activity shifted back to Glen Canyon. Outside

influences, included the financial panic of 1893, brought men to placer mining fields where, with little capital, they might make a self-reliant living. The election of President William McKinley in 1896 was a victory for those who supported the gold standard, and gold prices rose accordingly. Finally, the discovery of rich gold fields in the Klondike and Nome, Alaska, and in South Africa stimulated prospectors around the world.

By comparison, the gold boom in Glen Canyon was small, but unique. There were never more than a thousand men working the canyon at any one time. The best locations were found in the main canyon gravel terraces, some of them more than two hundred feet above the high-water mark. It was all placer gold; no coarse gold was ever found.

Recovering this fine gold dust taxed the patience and ingenuity of Glen Canyon miners, who used traditional sluice boxes and pans, as well as dredges and hydraulic hoses. Hydraulic mining was perhaps most difficult because most mines were above the river level and it was extremely difficult to get water where the miners needed it. Gravity diversion was virtually impossible because there were few tributary streams in the right places. Pumping water up from the river failed when sand and silt jammed and wore out the pumps. Miners at Good Hope Bar and Olympia Bar did have some success with water wheels, but they were the exception.

All told, miners tried out more than one hundred different types of patented mining machines, but the most reliable option remained the sluice and pan method. A few made thousands of dollars, and more made hundreds. But most miners obtained little more for their efforts than an exhilarating life in the great outdoors.

It was rugged country in which to travel. The canyons were real barriers to commerce. Wagon roads were opened to the Colorado River at key crossing points, including Lee's Ferry, Hite (Dandy) Crossing, Hall's Crossing, and Hole-in-the-Rock. More places were accessible by trail. Over these roads and trails, teamsters hauled in supplies and equipment, including foodstuffs from the peripheral Mormon farming communities, lumber and coal from the Henry Mountains, and other goods and tools from the railhead at Green River. In order to avoid Cataract Canyon, wagons hauled freight from Green River overland more than one hundred miles to Glen Canyon. Once supplies reached the riverbank, it was necessary to transport them by boat up or down the river to the diggings. Freighters used many kinds of boats, including scows, rafts, rowboats, skiffs, sailboats, and paddle wheel and propeller-driven steamboats.

Life for the canyon country gold miners was rough. Most men, and a few women, lived in tents, shacks, caves, or under the overhanging rock shelters. Dugouts and small rock houses were built in permanent locations. Lumber was expensive to bring in, and there was no local timber, but the resourceful miners were able to collect driftwood for building and for firewood. Above Lee's Ferry, the only place that could be called a community was Hite. A post office was located there, and one or another of the Hites operated a small store. Mail was brought in from Green River and carried from Hanksville to Hite on horseback.

West Canyon, Glen Canyon, Utah, ca. 1950s
Tad Nichols

Occasionally, trappers would work their way through the canyons during the winter and bring their furs out to Hite in the spring to process them. These visits from mountain men also served to remind the Glen Canyon miners just how far from civilization they really were.

STANTON'S GOLD DREDGE

After completing his railroad survey through the canyons of the Colorado in 1890, and failing to attract investors for the project, engineer Robert Brewster Stanton became involved in various railroad and mining projects in California, British Columbia, and Utah. He did not forget what he had observed in Glen Canyon, however, and in 1897 he finally persuaded some eastern capitalists to finance a gold dredging operation there.

Stanton envisioned Glen Canyon as a gigantic, natural sluice box with a streambed lined with gold. He planned to use a big, floating dredge of the type commonly employed throughout the West. If this pilot machine worked well, Stanton planned to install several others at different points in the canyon. He also imagined damming the tributaries, and the Colorado River itself, to generate electric power to operate the dredges.

Tests measured up to Stanton's expectations, and the Hoskaninni Company (named in honor of the Navajo headman who had first led Cass Hite to Glen Canyon in 1883) was formed in March 1898. As superintendent of field operations, Stanton ran further tests to determine the best place to install the first dredge. Then he began to stake out the canyon.

Stanton staked around pre-existing claims to ensure contiguity for his own claims. His ultimate goal was to mine the entire one hundred seventy miles of Glen Canyon, from the Dirty Devil River to Lee's Ferry. By the end of 1890, he had staked the entire canyon and filed one hundred forty-five separate claims in the recorders' offices of Garfield, Kane, and San Juan counties in Utah, and Coconino County in Arizona. At the same time, Stanton deployed workers to build roads, improve trails, and prepare to install several dredges at various points along the river. One crew did extensive work at Hole-in-the-Rock, cutting steps in the slickrock Mormon road to make it safer for pack animals.

In June 1890, the first dredge, manufactured by the Bucyrus Company, was delivered to the railhead at Green River. The parts were hauled by wagon to Hanksville, and from there to the river over a new road Stanton's men had cut. At the rim of Glen Canyon, Stanton's crew had to cut a dugway through the rock walls of a tributary canyon to get the equipment down to the river at Hall's Crossing. From there, the parts were floated four miles upstream to a place called Camp Stone, where they were reassembled.

The huge machine rested on a flat-bottomed hull one hundred fifty feet long, and consisted of a chain of 46 three-cubic-foot steel buckets and washing and amalgamating machinery. Five gasoline engines powered the entire contraption. The buckets scooped up sand and gravel from the river bottom and dumped it in a circular screen. Coarse gravel was carried away, and the remaining sand was washed over amalgamating tables to sift out the gold.

There were some mechanical failures at first—among other things, the boat would get stuck on the river bottom—but finally a general cleanup was made on April 13. The return: $30.15. Cleanup May 7: $36.80. These are the only figures given in the diary that Stanton kept during the life of the Hoskaninni Company. There must have been additional returns, but not many, because the elaborate sluicing and amalgamating machinery simply wasn't saving the fine gold dust.

Glen Canyon's gold defeated the big machine as it had most of the smaller ones.

The dredge ceased operations in the summer of 1901, and Stanton was made legal receiver of the company's property. He had no problem selling the company's horses, but finding a buyer for the rest of the property—dredge, claims, and all—was more difficult. Finally, Stanton found a buyer who was willing to pay $200 for the lot, and the Hoskaninni Company was dissolved.

The failed venture cost the Hoskaninni Company investors about $100,000. One of those

Roiling sky above the rim of Horseshoe Canyon, Utah LINDA CONNOR

investors, Julius Stone, came through the canyon on a river trip in 1938. Stone had served as the company's first president, and Camp Stone had been named for him. When Stone's party came upon the old dredge, beached and half-submerged, they decided to make camp. Salvaging some lumber from the ghostly barge, they built a fire and put on a pot of coffee. Savoring the moment, Stone told his companions all about the ill-fated Hoskaninni venture.

"This cup of coffee," he said, "cost me $5,000." It was the only return he ever got on his investment.

For another quarter century, the rusting Hoskaninni dredge remained visible at low water to remind Colorado River runners of a valiant attempt to mine the riches of Glen Canyon. The dredge and that ephemeral gold dust are there still, beneath the deep blue waters of Lake Powell.

SPENCER AND THE ZAHNS

The Glen Canyon gold rush petered out after the turn of the century. When Emery and Ellsworth Kolb passed through the canyon in 1911, en route from Green River, Wyoming, to Needles, California, they encountered only a few people. John Hite was still operating the post office at Hite Crossing. Bert Loper, who had worked claims along the San Juan, was living at the mouth of Red Canyon, and his nearest neighbor was Cass Hite, who lived across the river at Ticaboo. The Kolbs saw no one else until they came upon fifteen or twenty men who were building a large boat at the mouth of Warm Creek, twenty-eight miles upstream from Lee's Ferry. The men were working under the direction of Charles H. Spencer, canyon country mining entrepreneur.

Spencer hoped to achieve success where so many had tried, and failed, before. Among those who had been successful were brothers Hector and Otto Zahn, whose Los Angeles-based family had established the Zahn Mining Company in 1902. The company acquired promising property on both sides of the San Juan River, and set up an extensive sluicing operation, using heavy equipment that had been brought by the previous stakeholder from the railhead in Flagstaff, Arizona. The Zahns found enough placer gold to justify patenting the property, which they worked intermittently until World War I.

Access to the Zahn Camp was via a rough wagon road from Oljeto, down Copper Canyon and across the mouth of Nakai Canyon. Spencer built an even more primitive road off of the Zahn Camp road that led to his operation, four miles downstream. Spencer's idea was to recover embedded gold directly from the sandstone itself, rather than from the streambed. He brought in heavy machinery from Colorado by ox team and set up an elaborate rock crushing plant at the river's edge. But Spencer soon discovered that the quantities of recoverable gold embedded in the sandstone were exceedingly minute, and his machinery could not handle enough rock or save enough gold to make the operation pay.

He then became interested in the Chinle shales, which he first tested near Spencer Camp on the San Juan. Spencer found thick beds of this formation at Lee's Ferry on the Colorado, and determined to make his fortune from them. Notwithstanding the well-known and utter failure of the Hoskaninni Company dredging operation, Spencer was able to find enough investors to enable him to try his hand.

To provide fuel for steam-powered hydraulic and dredging equipment, Spencer developed coal prospects on upper Warm Creek, more than twenty miles upstream from the Colorado. He had to haul the coal in wagons to the mouth of the creek and then move it downstream to Lee's Ferry on a ninety-two-foot-long boat, dubbed the Charles H. Spencer, that he assembled on site.

Everything that could go wrong did. Spencer's eponymously named boat, the largest ever launched in Glen Canyon, was simply too big. It repeatedly got stuck on sand bars, and most of the coal hauled down to Lee's Ferry had to be consumed to power the boat back up, against the Colorado's swift current, to Warm Creek. The pneumatic dredges also did not work well because the Chinle shale was too sticky to sluice.

Spencer operated his mining operations at Lee's Ferry for less than a year, and abandoned the canyon in 1912. The gold boom was finally over.

When Clyde Eddy came through Glen Canyon in 1927, he saw only one person, William Carpenter,

living at Loper's Cabin at the mouth of Red Canyon. Once-populated sites such as Hite, Ticaboo, and Good Hope, Olympia, California, Boston, Gretchen, Schock and Klondike bars had become ghost camps on the Colorado.

THE CONQUEST

During the quarter century between 1896, when Utah achieved statehood, and 1922, when the Colorado River Compact was signed, the canyon country was subject to a series of economic booms as commercial interests sought to exploit other mineral and fossil fuel resources in the region.

Indians searching for turquoise inadvertently became the canyon country's first copper miners. While looking for the legendary Mitchell-Merrick mine in 1882, Cass Hite found copper deposits in Copper Canyon. That same year, Thomas Keams discovered some copper outcrops on the Kaibito Plateau. Other miners encountered copper associated with gold and silver ores in the La Sal, Abajo, and Henry mountains. But the largest

deposits were locked in the sandstone beds, often in proximity to radioactive minerals.

In 1898, gold prospectors in the La Sal Mountains discovered radioactive carnonite ore, and a new phase of canyon country mining began. The radium boom ended in 1924, followed by a vanadium boon, and finally a Cold War uranium boom.

The most significant industrial development in the canyon country began in 1882, when the Denver & Rio Grande Western Railroad began to tap the vast coal resources of the Wasatch Plateau and the Book Cliffs to supply its coal-fired locomotives. As the industry expanded and population increased, the territorial legislature carved Carbon County out of Emery County and designated Price as the new county seat. Annual coal production climbed steadily, taking a big jump during World War I and reaching six million tons in 1920.

The first oil well in canyon country was drilled near Green River in 1891, and E.L. Goodridge struck a small deposit of oil at Mexican Hat in 1908. However, further prospecting remained

Hall's Crossing on Lake Powell, Glen Canyon National Recreation Area, Utah KAREN HALVERSON

Edward Abbey taking notes at Turkey Pen Ruins, Grand Gulch Primitive Area, Utah MARK KLETT

somewhat fitful until after World War I, when the burgeoning automobile industry created an insatiable thirst for petroleum products. Throughout the 1920s, wells were drilled in Monument Valley, Elk Ridge, Beef Basin, Dark Canyon, along the Colorado River downstream from Moab, Robber's Roost, San Rafael Swell, Circle Cliffs, Glen Canyon, and Mexican Hat.

Notwithstanding all of this activity, the canyon country remained primarily a grazing and farming area. Once the limited agricultural land was taken up and the range divided, there was seemingly little potential for further growth. Following the passage of the anti-polygamy Edmunds-Tucker Law of 1882, the canyon country population did swell a bit as scores of Mormon families fled there to avoid prosecution for living according to the dictates of their conscience. Zealous United States

marshals found it difficult to rout out the "cohabs" from these areas. But resistance only provoked further federal legislation, and in 1896 polygamy was finally outlawed by the Church of Jesus Christ of Latter-day Saints and in the Utah constitution as a prerequisite for statehood.

In Navajo country south of the San Juan River, John Wetherill established a trading post at Oljeto to capitalize on the mining business and serve the Indians. Wetherill had come to the canyon country from southwestern Colorado, where he and his brothers had been the first non-Indians to explore and publicize the Ancestral Pueblo ruins at Mesa Verde. While running stock down the San Juan River and into Navajo country, Wetherill kept his eyes open for other ruins. Navajo guides he befriended eventually led him to the spectacular cliff dwellings of Betatakin, Keet Seel, and

Inscription House in Tsegi and Skeleton canyons, which are now preserved as units of Navajo National Monument.

In the summer of 1900, Henry N. Cowles and Joseph T. Hall opened a trading post at Hole-in-the-Rock, where for two years they did good business with Utes, Paiutes, and Navajos from as far away as Bluff, Navajo Mountain, and Tuba City. After Cowles and Hall abandoned the post, Navajos continued to use the Hole-in-the-Rock trail to trade with the Mormons at Escalante.

After completing his surveys of the Colorado Plateau, Maj. John Wesley Powell went to Washington and became the leading advocate for regional conservation and federally managed reclamation. Powell had seen how fundamentally important community-oriented irrigation was to the life of small Mormon villages. Based on his observations in Utah, he wrote *Arid Lands,* which offered the nation a blueprint for the development of the West. Cooperative enterprise was necessary to ensure the most efficient use of limited water, he said. As director of the U.S. Geological Survey, he initiated an irrigation survey of the West, and this was accompanied by unprecedented withdrawals of irrigable lands from the private sector.

With the National Reclamation Act of 1902, which set aside revenues from the sale of public lands to be used for reclamation purposes, and in subsequent legislation, the federal government embraced Powell's idea that "co-operative capital" was essential to the development of Western watersheds.

In the summer of 1905, the Colorado River spilled over its banks, flooded California's Imperial Valley fifty miles to the west, and created the Salton Sea. The breach was repaired with great difficulty the following year, but memories of the disaster lingered and helped motivate government agencies and private concerns to find ways to tame what was popularly called a "natural menace." Government agents and private concerns studied the river to determine how its waters might best be controlled for irrigation and hydroelectric power generation. In 1916, E.C. La Rue of the U.S. Geological Survey assembled the data in his paper, *Colorado River and Its Utilization,* which clearly indicated that dependence on the river was growing much faster in the lower basin than in the upper basin.

Legislators in the upper-basin states of Wyoming, Colorado, Utah, and Arizona were becoming apprehensive that users in the lower basin would establish prior rights, and some openly questioned whether individual states had the right to regulate the river's flow within or along their boundaries. Gradually, the various state legislatures agreed that a compact between the states was essential to the full development of the Colorado River. The best way for each state to secure its interests was to ensure that the rights of all were protected. In 1920, representatives from California, Arizona, Nevada, Utah, New Mexico, Colorado, and Wyoming initiated formal talks, and two years later the Colorado River Compact was signed.

The agreement divided the available water of the Colorado and its tributaries between the upper basin, north of Lee's Ferry, and the lower basin, and established a basis for future agreements between the Compact states. It also paved the way for federal legislation that would authorize construction of major multi-purpose projects. The Boulder Canyon Project Act passed in 1928 and led to the construction of Hoover Dam, while the Upper Colorado River Storage Act that authorized Glen Canyon Dam became law in 1956.

Symphony In Sandstone

BLANK VERSE

THE EXPLORER WHO LOOKS out over the canyon country from the rim of the Aquarius Plateau, who climbs about the lava cap of the rim, who enjoys a campfire and a sleep beneath the pine and spruce trees "forgets that he is a geologist and feels himself a poet." So wrote Capt. Clarence E. Dutton in Chapter XIII of his *Report on the Geology of the High Plateaus of Utah, with Atlas,* published in 1880 as part the U.S. Geographical and Geological Survey of the Rocky Mountain Region.

"The Aquarius should be described in blank verse and illustrated upon canvas," added Dutton, who was one of the few early explorers to describe the scenery of the canyon country in terms of the sublime. Father Escalante and Jacob Hamblin were articulate men of strong faith, but their accounts do not suggest that they sensed the hand of God at work in the landscape. Capt. John N. Macomb, looking toward the junction of the Green and Colorado rivers in 1859, saw a "worthless and impracticable region," while his companion, Dr. John Strong Newberry, described the view as "strange and beautiful."

Dutton's monographs are happy combinations of geology and belles lettres. Viewing the canyon country from the edge of the plateaus, he was compelled to depart from what he characterized as the "severe ascetic style which has become conventional in scientific monographs," and to describe the landscape aesthetically.

Petrified Sand Dunes, Paria Canyon-Vermilion Cliffs Wilderness, Arizona-Utah KERRY THALMANN

From the rim, what Dutton saw was not simply a laboratory of rocks but "a sublime panorama," and "an extreme of desolation, the blankest solitude, a superlative desert." At another vantage point, "The grandeur of the spectacle consists in a great number of cliffs rising successively one upon the other, like a stairway for the Titans, leading up to a mighty temple."

The works of the Powell, Wheeler, and Hayden surveys were enriched by contributions from photographers and illustrators whose work, quite as much as that of the authors, influenced the way we see the canyon country today. Subsequent official government publications lacked such inspiring illustrations.

The canyon country seemingly held little scenic attraction for those who struggled to eke out a meager living there. Ancestral Pueblo people most likely chose to build cliff dwellings because they offered defensive advantages rather than great views. Mormon villagers, trying to make a living from a narrow strip of marginal farmland, did not spend much time contemplating the aesthetics of their surroundings.

The cattlemen generally were slow to develop an appreciation for this intricate landscape, which offered so little grass and so many hollows in which cows could get lost. Indeed, during the pioneer period, those who most appreciated the canyon country were outlaws, "cohabs," and Indian raiders, all of whom found it a good place to hide out.

There is little in the written record to suggest that the gold miners had much interest in the natural scene, except as it offered clues as to where they might strike it rich. The outdoor life might have been appealing, but placer mining on the canyon bottoms was hard, and hardly rewarding, work. Nature was the adversary, and if the miners developed a grudging admiration for the landscape they didn't say so in writing.

BRIDGES OF STONE

In 1883, Cass Hite first saw the three natural stone bridges now preserved at Natural Bridges National Monument, but his account of the "discovery" was rather blasé. Located near the head of White

Colorado River and Canyonlands National Park from Dead Horse State Park, Utah GEORGE H.H. HUEY

Canyon, just below and west of the Bear's Ears on Elk Ridge, the bridges lie near the junction of two well-traveled cattle trails that approach the canyon country from the east and south. As such, various cowboys, including J.A. Scorup in 1895, visited the bridges.

In the spring of 1903, Scorup met Horace J. Long in Glen Canyon. Long was attempting to operate the abandoned Hoskaninni Company gold dredge for W.W. Dyar, the new owner. Long was that rare type of individual who took more interest in scenery than in the job at hand. When Scorup told Long about the stone bridges, the two men went to visit them. Long relayed his account of the trip to his employer, and the story was published in *Century Magazine* in August 1904. The following month's issue of *National Geographic Magazine* also carried a notice about "Colossal Natural Bridges in Utah."

These articles were among the first to extol the grandeur of the canyon country to a national audience, and they drew attention to a segment of the region that the Powell and Hayden surveys had largely passed over. Most Americans with a modicum of schooling were aware of Virginia's famous natural bridge, having seen illustrations of the span in their grammar school geography texts. The bridges in Utah were described as being so much larger than the Virginia bridge that the story seemed unbelievable.

In April 1905, a group sponsored by the Salt Lake Commercial Club visited the bridges. English born artist H.L.A. Culmer joined this party, took measurements, and made sketches on which to base his famous paintings. Photographs of the paintings of all three bridges were published in *National Geographic Magazine* in March 1907. In the accompanying article, E.F. Holmes advocated the establishment of a national park to protect these natural wonders, following the precedent set when Mesa Verde National Park and Petrified Forest National Monument were designated in 1906.

Culmer was a well-known landscape artist who admired the English painter Joseph M.W. Turner and the American artist Thomas Moran. His paintings reflect an understanding of geology as well as his profound love for the natural scene.

He found the eroded canyon country landscape of southeastern Utah stimulating and inspiring, and his paintings of the natural bridges, the arches later preserved in Arches National Park, the soaring formations of Monument Valley, and the San Rafael Swell endure as his best work.

Erosion "created scenes of magnificent disorder, in savage grandeur beyond description," Culmer wrote. "The remnants of the land remain of impressive but fantastic wildness, mute witnesses of the powers of frenzied elements, wrecking the world. These were the powers that fashioned those monoliths that rise like lofty monuments from the southern plains; that shaped those enormous stone bridges in the rim rock region of San Juan… and they strewed over a region as large as an empire such bewildering spectacles of mighty shapes that Utah must always be the land sought by explorers of the strange and marvelous."

Dyar and Holmes mentioned the existence of cliff dwellings in the vicinity of the bridges. This caught the attention of archeologists. In the summer of 1907, Dean Byron Cummings of the University of Utah School of Letters and Science, in cooperation with the Archeological Institute of America, organized a party to investigate the White Canyon bridges and the country north of the San Juan River. Cummings included data on the stone bridges in his report of the trip, which was sent to the General Land Office and brought to the attention of President Theodore Roosevelt. On April 16, 1908, Roosevelt established Natural Bridges National Monument, Utah's first.

That summer, Cummings returned to the San Juan region with a group of students to conduct an archeological dig at Alkali Ridge, west of Blanding. He took time out to join John Wetherill on a trip to visit Keet Seel, a massive, Ancestral Pueblo cliff dwelling ruin in the Tsegi Canyon system, a day's ride away from Wetherill's Oljeto trading post. Cummings' account came to the attention of W.B. Douglass, a government surveyor who had been assigned to map the formation of the new Natural Bridges National Monument. His report, in turn, provided the impetus for the new President, William Howard Taft, to designate Navajo National Monument on March 20, 1909.

Returning to Navajo country in the summer of 1909, and again guided by Wetherill, Cummings led an archeological expedition that investigated two more impressive cliff dwellings, Inscription House and Betatakin, on the Shonto Plateau and Tsegi Canyon, respectively. These, too, would be protected as units of the newly established Navajo National Monument.

After completing his archeological work, Cummings headed north to Navajo Mountain with Wetherill to find another natural bridge, about which they had heard reports from Paiute Indians. Along the way, they learned that Douglass, of the General Land Office, was also en route to look for the bridge. Joining forces, the Cummings and Douglass parties, led by Paiute guide Nasja-begay, skirted the rugged and dissected north side of Navajo Mountain. On August 14, 1909, the weary explorers stood before the magnificent arch of Rainbow Bridge.

Since 1882, if not before, miners had been combing the Navajo Mountain area searching for the fabled Mitchell-Merrick mine. Members of the Cummings-Douglass expedition saw evidence of mining activity at the mouths of Bridge and Aztec canyons on the Colorado River, five miles away from Rainbow Bridge. At least one miner, W.F. Williams, claimed to have first seen the huge stone span as early as 1884, but it was the Cummings-Douglass "discovery" in 1909 that directly led to national monument protection for Rainbow Bridge.

Douglass found that the arch soared 309 feet above the canyon creek bed and 235 feet above the canyon rims, upon which the bridge's abutments rested. The bridge spanned 279 feet, and at the highest point the stone arch was 42 feet thick and 33 feet wide. Despite its massive size, the bridge seems dwarfed by the broad canyon in which it resides, and by looming Navajo Mountain itself.

Douglass is credited with choosing the name "Rainbow Natural Bridge," which was suggested by the Paiute word, *barohoini,* for rainbow. The Navajos called the bridge *nonnezoshi,* which means great arch or great stone arch. On the basis of the report Douglass submitted to the General Land Office, and on an article Cummings published in the February 1910 issue of *National Geographic,*

President Howard Taft proclaimed Rainbow Bridge National Monument on May 30, 1910.

President Warren G. Harding proclaimed Hovenweep National Monument in 1923, and the same year, on the western edge of the canyon country, Congress established Bryce Canyon National Park. Capitol Reef National Monument was set aside in 1937, and elevated to National Park status in 1971.

CRESCENDO

Tourist travel to the eastern side of the canyon country began almost as soon as Natural Bridges, Navajo, and Rainbow Bridge national monuments were created and publicized. John and Louisa Wade Wetherill moved their trading business from Oljeto to Kayenta in 1910, and for the next thirty-three years their trading post served as a base for archeological and exploratory expeditions and tourist trips throughout the Navajo country south of the San Juan. John Wetherill, who led most of these expeditions himself, also became the first custodian of Navajo National Monument in the 1930s. North of the San Juan, Blanding resident Ezekiel "Zeke" Johnson handled pack trips to the natural bridges and through the country west of the Clay Hills. Johnson also served as the first custodian of Natural Bridges National Monument.

Although it was the least accessible of the three monuments, Rainbow Bridge became the most popular attraction. Among the more notable visitors whom Wetherill escorted to the bridge in 1913 were former President Theodore Roosevelt and Western author Zane Gray. Over the next decade, Gray would return to Rainbow Bridge again and again. His autobiographical *Tales of Lonely Trails,* published in 1922, opens with his account of a trip to Rainbow Bridge. That book, and best-selling novels such as *Riders of the Purple Sage, Rainbow Trail, Heritage of the Desert, The Vanishing American,* and *Wildfire,* vividly convey Gray's great affection for the landscape of the canyon country.

"I love wild canyons—dry, fragrant, stone-walled, with their green-choked niches and gold-tipped ramparts," Gray wrote.

Between 1920 and 1930, Charles L. Bernheimer conducted several explorations of Navajo country and the area north of the San Juan. Bernheimer, who described himself as "a tenderfoot and a cliff-dweller from Manhattan," was drawn to the canyon country by the writings of Zane Gray. He employed both Wetherill and Johnson to guide him, but insisted in going beyond the well-traveled routes and into new areas. His notes contributed significantly to our knowledge of the geography and human prehistory of the area.

On a 1921 expedition, Bernheimer tried unsuccessfully to locate the Crossing of the Fathers, which had been all but forgotten by the local population. The following year, outfitted with a pack train, he circumnavigated Navajo Mountain and visited Rainbow Bridge. Bernheimer published fascinating accounts of his experiences in articles for *Natural History* and *National Geographic* magazines, and in his aptly titled 1924 book, *Rainbow Bridge: Circling Navajo Mountain and Explorations in the "Bad Lands" of Southern Utah and Northern Arizona.*

After World War I the automobile came of age, and many tourists opted to travel by car rather than by train. However, the only roads in the canyon country were those that connected the small settlements on the periphery and most of these were better suited for horse-drawn wagons than for private automobiles. Therefore, most canyon country tourists opted to take the train and travel to the more remote areas on horseback.

The U.S. Geological Survey issued a series of official *Guidebooks of the Western United States* that were helpful to tourists traveling on the various transcontinental railroad lines. These included detailed maps, geological data, and other interpretive information. Those of most interest to canyon country visitors were *The Santa Fe Route with a Side Trip to the Grand Canyon of the Colorado,* by Nelson Darton, and *The Denver & Rio Grande Western Route,* by Marius Campbell.

The Santa Fe Railway, along with the Fred Harvey Company, heavily advertised the Grand Canyon and promoted Harveycar Indian Detours. Closer at hand, the Denver & Rio Grande Western publicized the scenic attractions along its line,

Grosvenor Arch, Grand Staircase-Escalante National Monument, Utah GEORGE H.H. HUEY

including the Book Cliffs and Castle Gate at the mouth of Price Canyon. The railroad's promotional literature also included poetry and stories, with titles such as "Valley Tan," "Ticaboo," and "Hoskaninni," written by former gold miner and *New York Sun* reporter Cy Warman, "Poet of the Rockies."

Frederick S. Dellenbaugh published his seminal work, *Romance of the Colorado,* in 1902, the same year that Congress passed the National Reclamation Act. This book, along with Dellenbaugh's follow-up volume, *A Cañon Voyage,* published in 1908, greatly stimulated interest in running the Colorado River for pleasure. Julius Stone, who had lost his investment in Robert Brewster Stanton's erstwhile Hoskaninni gold mining venture, was motivated to make his 1909 river trip as much from reading Dellenbaugh's books as from Stanton's reports.

And photographers Ellsworth and Emery Kolb, who in 1911–12 became the first men to film the canyons of the Colorado, used Dellenbaugh's *A Cañon Voyage* as their guide.

The first commercial tours of Glen Canyon began in 1917, when David E. Rust started taking tour groups form North Wash to Lee's Ferry using folding, two-person, canvas-covered boats. By the time Norman Nevills began river-running trips on the San Juan in the 1930s, the fate of both rivers had been sealed.

In 1921, the U.S. Geological Survey and the Southern California Edison Company conducted research that would help shape the Colorado River Compact and lay the groundwork for construction of Glen Canyon Dam and the creation of the Lake Powell reservoir. Teams carefully mapped the canyons of the Colorado from the head of

San Juan River and Monument Valley from Muley Point, Utah   W. Ross Humphreys

Cataract to Lee's Ferry, and San Juan River canyon from the mouth of Chinle Creek. One group of surveyors, led by K.W. Trimble, hiked up to Rainbow Bridge National Monument from the Colorado River to determine whether the reservoir being envisioned would threaten the monument.

The following year, Dr. John Widtsoe, en route to Santa Fe to represent Utah in signing the Colorado River Compact, toured Glen Canyon along with a distinguished group of officials from the U.S. Geological Survey and Bureau of Reclamation. Their ostensible objective was to look at the most suitable site for a hydroelectric dam. The party, led by geologist E.C. La Rue, entered the river at Hall's Crossing and saw the Hole-in-the-Rock Crossing, Rainbow Bridge, the Crossing of the Fathers, and other landmarks.

"I quite agree with Major Powell," Widstoe wrote in his diary of the voyage. "…it is useless to describe with words or even with pictures the wonders, of surprising magnitude and beauty, that fill the country through which we have passed on this trip."

Widstoe could just as well have been speaking for the whole sweep of country from the Book Cliffs in Utah to White Mesa in Arizona, and from Bryce Canyon to the Four Corners—an area of unparalleled grandeur and one of the earth's great places. Certainly he would have concurred with the words of anthropologist T. Mitchell Prudden, who called the entire Colorado Plateau "the world's masterpiece."

Claret Cup Cactus, Lavender Canyon near Canyonlands National Park, Utah BILL ELLZEY

SUGGESTED
READING

Abbey, Edward. *Desert Solitaire: A Season in the Wilderness* [1968] Reprint. New York: Ballentine Books, 1991.

Baars, Donald L. *Canyonlands Country: Geology of Canyonlands and Arches National Parks.* Salt Lake City: University of Utah Press, 1994.

Collier, Michael. *Water, Earth and Sky: The Colorado River Basin.* Salt Lake City: University of Utah Press, 1999.

Crawford, John L. *Zion National Park: Towers of Stone.* Springdale, UT: Zion Natural History Association, 1995.

Dellenbaugh, Frederick Samuel. *The Romance of the Colorado River.* [1902] New York: Dover Publications, Inc., 1998.

Escalante, Francisco Silvestre Velez de. *The Dominguez-Escalante Journal: Their Expedition Through Colorado, Utah, Arizona, and New Mexico, 1776.* Salt Lake City: University of Utah Press, 1995.

Farmer, Jared. *Glen Canyon Dammed: Inventing Lake Powell and the Canyon Country.* Tucson: University of Arizona Press, 1999.

Hassell, Hank. *Rainbow Bridge: An Illustrated History.* Logan: Utah State University, 1999.

Jennings, Jesse. *Glen Canyon: An Archeological Summary.* Salt Lake City: University of Utah Press, 1998.

Leach, Nicky J. *The Guide to National Parks of the Southwest.* [1992] Revised edition. Tucson: Southwest Parks and Monuments Association, 1999.

Lee, Katie. *All My Rivers Are Gone: A Journey of Discovery Through Glen Canyon.* Boulder, CO: Johnson Books, 1998.

Lister, Florence C. and Robert H. Lister. *Those Who Came Before: Southwestern Archeology in the National Park System* [1983] Revised edition. Tucson: Southwest Parks and Monuments Association, 1994.

Negri, Richard F. *Tales of Canyonlands Cowboys.* Ogden: Utah State University Press, 1997.

Nichols, Tad. *Glen Canyon: Images of a Lost World.* Santa Fe: Museum of New Mexico Press, 1999.

Porter, Eliot. *The Place No One Knew: Glen Canyon on the Colorado* [1963] Revised edition. Layton, Utah: Gibbs Smith Publisher, 2000.

Powell, John Wesley. *The Exploration of the Colorado River and its Canyons.* New York: Viking Penguin, 1997.

Reilly, P.T. and Robert Webb. *Lees Ferry: From Mormon Crossing to National Park.* Logan: Utah State University Press, 1999.

Stegner, Wallace Earle. *Beyond the Hundredth Meridian: John Wesley Powell and the Second Opening of the West* [1954] Reprint. New York: Viking Penguin, 1992.

ILLUSTRATION CREDITS

INDEX